The Racial Profiling Controversy

Brian L. Withrow

Looseleaf
Law Publications, Inc.

43-08 162nd Street
Flushing, NY 11358
www.LooseleafLaw.com
800-647-5547

This publication is not intended to replace nor be a substitute for any official procedural material issued by your agency of employment nor other official source. Looseleaf Law Publications, Inc., the author and any associated advisors have made all possible efforts to ensure the accuracy and thoroughness of the information provided herein but accept no liability whatsoever for injury, legal action or other adverse results following the application or adoption of the information contained in this book.

Library of Congress Cataloging-in-Publication Data

Withrow, Brian L.
  Racial profiling controversy : what every police leader should know / by Brian L. Withrow.
      p. cm.
  Includes bibliographical references and index.
  ISBN 978-1-932777-91-8 (alk. paper)
  1. Racial profiling in law enforcement--United States. 2. Criminal justice, Administration of--United States. I. Title.
  HV8141.W578 2011
  363.2'308900973--dc22
                                                2010032111

Cover design by *Sans Serif, Inc.,* Saline, Michigan

Ten Things Policing Leaders Should Know About Racial Profiling

When you have finished this book, you should have a thorough understanding of these key areas:

- ➤ The structure of racial profiling research—How do we know what we know?

- ➤ How racial profiling data is (or should be) collected and consumed.

- ➤ The importance of managing discretion and controlling consent searches.

- ➤ The trap of deployment and the risks of disengagement.

- ➤ How to win a court challenge.

- ➤ The importance of enforcing the whole law.

- ➤ Why officers should stick to the script and close the deal.

- ➤ Your message matters.

- ➤ Diversity (in all its forms) makes you stronger.

- ➤ Respond proactively to allegations of racial profiling.

Dedication

To my Dad
M. L. "Buck" Withrow. Jr.
The smartest cop I know.

Table of Contents

Atticus Analytics

"Research Analysis Knowledge Solutions"

Atticus Analytics is a full service consulting firm dedicated to improving the quality of life in our clients' communities. We provide high quality research and analytical services to produce the knowledge essential for solving problems. Most of our clients are police departments, criminal justice agencies and allied organizations. We also provide litigation assistance and expert testimony on a broad range of policing systems and practices, with a particular emphasis on racial profiling.

We believe in common sense solutions. Our clients call us when they need the objectivity and technical skills only an independent consultant can provide. Our commitment to clients is uncomplicated. We only accept consultations when we are qualified. We fully disclose our fees and charges, up front. We adhere to our client's schedule. We guarantee our work. In fact, we are the only firm we know of that offers a money back guarantee.

We invite you to learn more about Atticus Analytics. Call our Principal, Dr. Brian L. Withrow, directly at 512-779-4125 or visit our website at www.atticusanalytics.com. Look under the Resources tab to find examples of our work.

Dr. Brian L. Withrow, Principal
brian.withrow@atticusanalytics.com
www.atticusanalytics.com
512-779-4125

About the Author

D r. Withrow is one of the nation's leading experts on the racial profiling controversy. He has authored numerous articles and reports on this issue. Dr. Withrow's 2006 publication, *Racial Profiling: From Rhetoric to Reason* (Pearson/Prentice Hall) is one of the most widely read textbooks on racial profiling. Because of his professional experience as a police administrator and extensive research as a scholar, Dr. Withrow is regularly asked to provide technical and litigation assistance to police agencies.

He is the founder and principal of Atticus Analytics and an Associate Professor of Criminal Justice at Texas State University - San Marcos. Prior to joining the Texas State University faculty in 2009, Brian was an Associate Professor and Director of the Forensic Sciences Program at Wichita State University. While on the faculty at Wichita State University, he served one term as Mayor of Bel Aire, Kansas. From 1993 to 1999, Dr. Withrow managed a police leadership development program at Sam Houston State University in Huntsville, Texas. From 1981 to 1993, Brian worked for the Texas Department of Public Safety as a State Trooper, Training Officer, Inspector and Bureau Manager.

Brian earned his Bachelor of Arts degree in Criminal Justice from Stephen F. Austin State University in 1981, his Masters of Public Administration from Southwest Texas State University in 1993, and his Doctor of Philosophy in Criminal Justice from Sam Houston State University in 1999.

Residing in Austin Texas, he is an Eagle Scout, has remained active in the Boy Scouts of America throughout his life and currently serves as a Unit Commissioner for the Capitol Area Council, BSA. He and his wife Lisa (an elementary school teacher and children's book author) have been married for 27 years and have four grown children.

Preface

 f you spend enough time in any single profession eventually, you see ironies that baffle younger colleagues. Such was the case during the summer of 2009 as I was writing this text.

On July 16, 2009, Patricia Whalen was taking a walk during her lunch hour when she observed two men attempting to break into a house. Thinking the men were burglarizing the house she dialed 911. Sergeant James Crowley of the Cambridge Police Department responded to the call. When he arrived at the scene, he observed an "older black man in the foyer" of the house. He later learned this man, Professor Henry Louis Gates, Jr., had "broken" into his own home because his key would not work in the lock. What happened next is unclear; however, we do know these two men engaged in a rather heated argument. A portion of this argument happened on the porch in front of curious onlookers. That was enough for Sergeant Crowley to arrest Dr. Gates. Eventually the charge (disorderly conduct) was dropped but by that time the event captured the attention of the entire nation.

There are three ironies in this story. First, one of the world's leading scholars on race, and the person who in 1995 actually coined the term "driving while Black," was alleging to be a victim of racial profiling. Second, according to CNN, Sergeant Crowley "had once been chosen by a black police officer to teach a police academy course on ways to avoid racial profiling." Third, in her 911 call to report what she reasonably believed to be a burglary, Ms. Whalen never mentioned the race of the men attempting to enter the house.

At best the two men involved in this incident thought the worst of each other. Dr. Gates thought Sergeant Crowley was a racist. Sergeant Crowley thought Dr. Gates was a burglar. Under normal circumstances this incident would have eventually faded away into a historical footnote. Unfortunately, less than a week later during a nationally televised press conference President Barack Obama described this incident as a "teachable moment." Even then, most of us would have likely agreed. This incident reminded us that we Americans have never really been comfortable with our racial differences. Then regrettably, President Obama characterized the behavior of the Cambridge Police Department by stating they "acted stupidly." The magnifying lens of the 24-hour news cycle then focused on the incident. By the end of it Sergeant Crowley and Professor Gates emerged relatively unscathed and have since even met again socially. Not so for the new president. He later apologized for commenting on a local issue without knowing the facts. Although that did not keep him from being criticized for serving *imported* beer during a Rose Garden Beer Summit hastily called to resolve the differences between Sergeant Crowley and Professor Gates.

For the past sixteen years I have spent countless hours in classrooms, conference rooms, training academies, association meetings, police departments and courtrooms dissecting racial profiling issues. In the nearly thirty years I have been actively involved in policing, as a police officer, administrator and now a university professor, I cannot recall another controversy that has caused so much grief for so many people for so long. Racial profiling is an emotionally divisive issue that shows no signs of slowing down. In fact, there is compelling evidence that within the next few years we will see a resurgence of litigation and racial profiling studies involving police departments as well as in other environments.

Through these experiences I have learned a few important lessons.
> — *Policing leaders really want to address the racial profiling controversy more proactively. American policing is moving beyond its initial defiance and has begun responding to the racial profiling controversy on its own terms.*

> — *Some of the most important racial profiling research exists within the ivory towers of academia. The racial profiling research agenda is maturing yet it remains largely inaccessible to most policing practitioners. There is a real need to compile this research into a format that will inform policy and guide practice.*

> — *Policing leaders are weary of the rhetoric and political correctness within the racial profiling controversy. They've watched their colleagues get hammered by the media and advocacy groups over the most innocuous statements and policy decisions. They've watched their officers struggle with racial profiling accusations arising out of the most benign traffic stops.*

> — *Even the most carefully planned and accurately analyzed racial profiling studies do not change minds.*

Consistently I have observed that when presented with the same set of facts (or research findings), attitudes toward the police seldom change. Supporters of the police remain supportive and critics of the police remain critical. Nothing changes.

These are the reasons I wrote this book.

The purpose of *The Racial Profiling Controversy: What Every Police Leader Should Know* is to provide policing leaders with access to the information they need in a format they can use to respond proactively to the racial profiling controversy. There is no agenda, political correctness or social commentary. This text neither accuses nor defends, it merely reports and informs. In doing so, controversy is quite likely. I fully expect to be taken to task by plaintiff's attorneys, questioned by my students and even criticized by my police chief friends over some of the passages I've written. So be it. After all, a little controversy is a good thing, isn't it?

The introduction contains a brief history and explains how six seemingly unrelated events combined to form the racial profiling controversy. Following this is a summary of hundreds of racial profiling studies conducted nationwide. This comprehensive analysis reveals several surprising patterns that contradict many of the widely reported myths within the racial profiling controversy.

The next chapters include the ten most important issues within racial profiling research and litigation. These chapters are intended to be brief and where possible they are presented in outline format to allow the reader to "brush up" on a particular dimension of the racial profiling controversy as it becomes relevant to them. For example, Chapters One (The Structure of Racial Profiling Research—How do We Know What We Know?) and Two (How Racial Profiling Data Is (or Should Be) Collected and Consumed) would be particularly useful to a department planning or responding to a racial profiling study. Chapter Five (How to Win a Court Challenge) might be helpful to a department facing a racial profiling lawsuit.

The lack of volume within these pages should not be construed to mean that the treatise is not comprehensive. The brevity of the material is by design. Policing leaders are busy people and do not have the time to review thousands of pages of academic research. This textbook was written specifically to communicate a great deal of information about an incredibly complicated topic in as concise a manner is ethically possible.

Because many of the important issues relating to the racial profiling controversy are interrelated the reader may notice some repetition throughout the textbook. Again, this is by design. Some issues transcend several dimensions of the racial profiling controversy. For example the power dynamics of the traffic stop/consent search is extremely important within several dimensions of the racial profiling controversy. As a result, this issue is discussed within the context of several chapters. The reason for this repetition, which is something that is frowned upon in traditional academic textbooks, is simple. Policing practitioners need a resource they can access quickly and be assured that they are well informed of the various aspects of the issue.

The concluding chapter (Final Thoughts) discusses the potential future of the racial profiling controversy. The racial profiling controversy began within the context of the traffic stop. Today the controversy is relevant in asset protection (shoplifting), air travel and even immigration enforcement at the local level. Importantly, the social costs of the racial profiling controversy that threaten the viability of the criminal justice system are discussed in this final section.

In addition to the usual tables and figures found in many textbooks, this textbook includes an extensive collection of illustrations and analogies. ***These features are designed to accomplish two important objectives.*** *First,* illustrations facilitate the learning process. The information contained in these features is intended to be more accessible than it normally would be if it were contained within large blocks of uninterrupted paragraphs. *Second,* analogies are effective communications tools. Complicated issues are easier to understand when presented in a familiar context.

Finally, at the risk of alienating my colleagues in sheriffs' departments, state agencies and other non-municipal law enforcement agencies I have chosen to use the terms policing, police departments, policing leaders, etc. This in no way should be interpreted to mean that I am ignoring these agencies. My use of these terms represents a personal bias. We are in the habit of referring to the policing function as "law enforcement." I believe this is a mistake. Policing is much larger than law enforcement.

Brian L. Withrow, Ph.D.
Austin, Texas
December 2009

Introduction

The Emergence of a Controversy

Controversies are essentially disagreements over a contentious topic. Participants in a controversy have strong feelings and are often quite willing to express them. Beyond disagreements and strong feelings, controversies are controversial precisely because the conflicts within them are seemingly irreconcilable. Unless and until someone with perceived legitimacy steps forward and offers a workable compromise, an issue will remain controversial as long as the parties concerned are willing to hold forth.

In order for a controversy to grow it must first have a name. Names and labels help the participants in a controversy communicate meanings. For example, for decades the foreign nationals that lived and worked in the United States without permission were referred to as "undocumented workers" or "illegal aliens." Today, these individuals are referred to merely as "illegals," suggesting their total presence in the country is illegitimate and wrong. A commentary on the current immigration controversy is well beyond the scope of this book. The point here is that regardless of where a person's opinion falls within this controversy, there are important semantic and connotative differences between the terms "undocumented worker" and "illegal." Putting it another way, words have meaning and are intended to invoke a response. The terms used to describe racial profiling are just as descriptive, and equally offensive.

Controversies don't just happen. More often than not, a controversy is the next iteration of a series of events, a convergence of various related factors, or both. When the racial profiling controversy is analyzed within a historical context, we see that there is really little of it that is new. In fact, from one perspective the racial profiling controversy can be viewed as the next iteration of racial conflict that has plagued our nation since its founding. However, from another perspective, the racial profiling controversy may be viewed as a convergence of events that coalesced into a single controversy.

Finally, the best way to begin resolving a controversy is to objectively consider the facts. More specifically, the participants in a controversy should determine where they agree,

1

where they disagree, and on what they agree to disagree. Participants on both sides of the racial profiling controversy have a habit of expressing rhetorical statements as fact. We are amused, but not surprised, by the newspaper columnist's line in the movie *The Man Who Shot Liberty Valance*, "When the legend becomes fact, print the legend." Unfortunately, reporting the legend as fact does not advance the controversy toward a resolution. It is important at the outset of this text to separate what we know from what we don't know.

Creating "Racial Profiling"

The racial profiling controversy, as we know it today, began in earnest in 1995 following the publication of the first large-scale racial profiling study on the New Jersey Turnpike. The term "racial profiling" first appeared seven years earlier (October 8, 1987) in a *San Diego Tribune* story about a major drug seizure in Utah. By October 23, 1995, Henry Louis Gates had coined the term "driving while Black" in an article appearing in *The New Yorker* (Heumann and Cassak 2003). Along the way similar terms, such as, "driving while Brown," "flying while Arab," "shopping while Black," and even "working while illegal," have been used broadly to describe an alleged pattern of behavior wherein the police focus their enforcement attention onto an individual because of that individual's race or ethnicity.

A Convergence of Events

One could reasonably argue that the racial profiling controversy is merely the next iteration of a long-standing conflict between racial groups, socioeconomic classes and the police. Racial and class conflicts are neither new nor distinctly American. Indeed they are as old as humanity itself. Two factors distinguish the racial profiling controversy from similar quarrels. First, unlike previous conflicts of a similar nature, the racial profiling controversy has an enduring quality. The controversy began within the context of the ubiquitous traffic stop. Today, we see elements of the controversy in many other contexts, including traveling, shopping, working and even education. Second, the racial profiling controversy is the result of a convergence of six unrelated factors. At the time of this convergence, two of these factors had been controversial for decades. As a result, these two factors were foundational in the sense that the racial profiling controversy would not likely have happened without them. The remaining four all happened during the mid-1990s. The convergence of the following six factors was the impetus for the racial profiling controversy (see Figure One).

Figure One – *Factors contributing to the racial profiling controversy.*

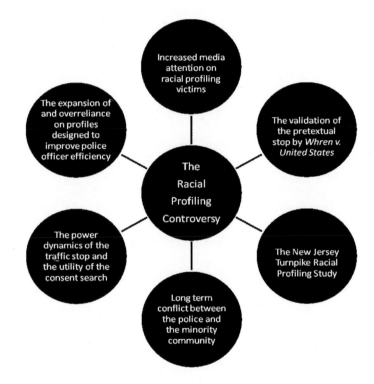

Conflict between the police and the minority community certainly predates the current racial profiling controversy. The history of American policing includes many examples of this conflict, particularly during the Civil Rights Era in the middle part of the 20th century. It is upon this foundation that the racial profiling controversy emerged.

Active research into the effect race/ethnicity plays in police decision making started in the 1970s. This research attempted to determine whether an individual's race/ethnicity influences a police officer's enforcement decision, e.g., to warn, cite, or arrest. Generally, this research finds that an individual's race/ethnicity has very little influence on a police officer's enforcement decision (Bittner, 1970, Black 1971, 1976, 1980; Black and Reiss 1970; Quinney 1980; Rubenstein 193; Smith and Visher 1981; Van Maanen 1974). It would seem this finding would be relevant to the racial profiling controversy. After all, if these researchers consistently find that police offices are only nominally influenced by an individual's race/ethnicity then how can the police be accused of racial profiling? The difference is that all of the previous researchers studied well-documented cases wherein the race/ethnicity of the individual was known to the police, such as during a call for service or while investigating reported crime. **None of the previous researchers attempted to determine whether an individual's race/ethnicity affects a police officer's decision to initiate an enforcement action, e.g., a stop.**

Citizen surveys consistently report that support for the police is lower within the minority community (Walker, Spohn and DeLone 2000). Minorities are less likely to view police stops as legitimate (Cole, 1999; Lundman and Kaufman 2003; Ramirez, McDevitt and Farrell 2000; Weitzer and Tuch 2002; Withrow and Jackson 2002), more likely to allege that they are singled out by the police (Tomaskovic-Devey, Mason and Zingraff 2004), and more willing to interpret aspects of a police stop as racially motivated than non-minorities (Fridell et al. 2001; Withrow and Jackson 2002). **These findings should not, however, be interpreted to mean that there is a lack of support for the police within the minority community.** Generally, the majority of all people regardless of their race or ethnicity support the police. The typical survey finds that support for the police may be seventy percent among non-minority residents and sixty percent among minority residents. There are very few documented cases where the majority of individuals from one race/ethnic group report an unfavorable opinion of the police.

Finally, some of this conflict is actually, but innocently, caused by proactive policing. In the current community/problem oriented era police departments often seek opportunities to proactively address crime. Sometimes the residents in high crime areas (often predominantly minority) request police assistance with neighborhood blight, gang warfare, and drug-trafficking problems. The police are usually willing to help, but in doing so may sow the seeds of conflict. For `example, saturation patrol and active code enforcement strategies may sufficiently interrupt criminal activities resulting in an overall reduction, or at least a displacement, of crime. Unfortunately, the individuals subjected to these aggressive strategies are often the resident of the very community that requested this level of intervention. Sometimes when the results of these strategies materialize it may appear that the police are targeting a particular portion of the community, usually the minority community. Of course, they are. This police attention is not, however, caused by racism. The police are there because they were asked to be there. Over time the initial request for assistance is forgotten only to be replaced by an accusation of racial profiling.

The power dynamics of the traffic stop and the utility of the consent search are also part of the foundation upon which the racial profiling controversy emerged. The traffic stop is the most ubiquitous event in criminal justice. The majority of policing enforcement actions, and therefore criminal proceedings, start with the deceptively routine traffic stop. The overall quality of a department's enforcement program, and particularly drug interdiction, is dependent upon police officers making a lot of traffic stops. A large proportion of appellate court rulings on Constitutional questions in criminal justice, including the leading case in racial profiling, arose from a traffic stop context.

Nearly every police department has a policy on *how* to conduct a traffic stop. Some of these policies even require officers to follow a specific script, notify the dispatch office upon initiating the stop, and even to report when the officer has stopped a prominent person in the community. With the exception of policies requiring officers to stop impaired or particularly flagrant violators, very few departments provide direction to their officers on *who, what, when, where,* and *why* to initiate a traffic stop. This provides officers with substantial discretion and the vast majority of these officers use this discretion wisely.

Unfortunately, the traffic stop is the source of most citizen complaints, and most of these, according to an experienced police chief who prefers to remain anonymous, "Happen because the officer forgets the last step of the violator contact," which of course is "Leave." Within the context of the racial profiling controversy, the traffic stop includes a controversial power dynamic.

This power dynamic is based on the following assumptions:

- The traffic code provides a nearly inexhaustible number of potential violations, for which a violator may be legally stopped.

- Most drivers, when followed long enough (and usually not very long), will violate at least one traffic law.

- When stopped, most drivers (even those who either know they don't have to or are aware that they are in possession of contraband) will, when asked, consent to a search.

This power dynamic sets the stage for the *pretextual stop*. A pretextual stop is a traffic stop justified by a bona fide violation of the law, but actually motivated by an unsupported suspicion of a more serious criminal violation. The typical pretextual stop begins when a police officer observes a "suspicious" driver/vehicle but cannot articulate a probable cause for initiating the stop. The officer will then follow the vehicle until the driver commits a traffic violation, usually a relatively minor infraction. Upon observing the violation, the officer will initiate the stop. Very soon during the stop the officer may ignore the initial violation and ask the driver for consent to search. There is absolutely nothing illegal about this practice. In fact, some police administrators may even consider this practice an effective interdiction or crime suppression tool.

It is, however, precisely the frequency of such stops involving minority drivers, the routine overlooking of the traffic violation and the early timing of the consent search request that lead critics of the police to perceive these stops as racially motivated. An African-American physician, once interviewed by the author during another research project stated this more succinctly: "I get stopped a dozen times a year in my Mercedes when I go to visit my mother back in the hood, but I never get a ticket and I am always asked to consent to a search. I get the feeling the police are interested in something more than my bad driving."

The expansion of and over reliance on profiles designed to improve police officer efficiency contributed to the racial profiling controversy.

"Profiling is the use of a combination of physical, behavioral, or psychological factors that, after being subjected to careful analysis improves the probability of identifying and apprehending a suspect."

—Withrow 2006:14–5

There are various types of profiles. Criminal profiles, made famous in the film *The Silence of the Lambs*, were developed as an investigatory tool to facilitate the identification of an offender. Criminal profiling differs from racial profiling by virtue of the fact that the criminal profile is developed after a crime has been committed. Racial profiles, to the extent they exist, are more like the hijacker profiles developed in the late 1960s to identify potential airline hijackers. These profiles relied on various demographic and behavioral clues to identify an individual's potential for violating the law.

Racial profiling has its origins in drug courier profiling, which was designed to improve a police officer's ability to interdict the distribution of illegal drugs. Drug courier profiles were originally developed in the mid-1970s by the United States Drug Enforcement Administration for use in the nation's airports. By 1985, the Florida Department of Motor Vehicles developed the first formal drug courier profiles for use in a traffic enforcement context (Engel, Calnon, and Bernard 2002; Harris 2002; Heumann and Cassak 2003). There is nearly no empirical evidence that drug courier profiles actually increase an officer's capacity to identify and interdict illegal drug trafficking. That, however, does not mean that they are ineffective. Policing leaders are encouraged to use any tool available to improve officer efficiency.

With respect to drug interdiction, policing leaders are especially encouraged to support drug courier profiles because:

- Illegal drug use has for decades been justifiably perceived to be the most serious threat to public safety,
- Police departments, often encouraged by political leaders, are highly motivated to vigorously enforce drug laws,
- Police departments are rewarded for drug seizures, both with additional appropriations from appreciative political leaders and through the asset forfeiture process, and
- Police officers are publically recognized and rewarded for significant drug and asset seizures.

After all, when was the last time you saw a police officer's picture on the front page of the local newspaper receiving an award for issuing a good speeding ticket? What officer would ignore a technique that promises to improve his ability to identify drug couriers and eventually lead to a promotion?

Of course, at least initially, none of this had anything at all to do with racial profiling. The original drug courier profiles did not explicitly encourage police officers to focus their attention onto racial/ethnic minorities. Instead it is more likely that race/ethnic specific factors crept their way into drug courier profiles through various training programs and intelligence reports that suggested drug couriers are more likely to be racial/ethnic minorities (Carter and Katz-Bannister 2004; Cole 1999; Donzinger 1996; Harris 2002; Leitzel 2001; Tonry 1995; United States General Accounting Office 2000; Walker, Spohn, and DeLone 2000).

Media attention, beginning in the mid-1990s, contributed to the racial profiling controversy by increasing public awareness. This in turn encouraged political leaders, who also have legitimate authority over policing organizations, to respond. Feature stories on racial profiling are particularly newsworthy when the alleged victim is either seemingly "honorable" or if the police officer's explanation is contrary to the facts. Stories about successful minority professionals who are frequently stopped suggest that the police are motivated by a suspicion, based on a racist's notion, that minorities driving expensive cars are likely drug dealers. One of the most infamous of these stories involved the police shooting of four African-American youths during a "routine" traffic stop. The youths were on their way home from a church-sponsored activity. One of the bullets actually lodged in a Bible that was on the dashboard. Sometimes the police attempt to justify the stop by stating that the driver or vehicle fit the description of a known suspect. If true, the story would likely not be newsworthy. After all, aren't the police supposed to do that? Unfortunately, in some cases, the police are unable to either produce a similar description or offer a description that is markedly different from the one they allege motivated the stop.

While the stops described in these stories are far from representative of the millions of police/citizen encounters that occur annually, they do share a few common characteristics.

First, the stops described in these stories are decidedly harsher and more punitive than what the situation appears to justify.

Second, the stops portrayed in these stories tend to be more protracted and invasive than the usual traffic stop.

Third, the individuals alleging to be victims of racial profiling report that they are stopped frequently, or at least more frequently than most people (e.g., non-minorities) are stopped.

The decision in *Whren v. United States* validated a well-established police practice, i.e., the pretextual stop, that is believed to be an important mechanism for racial profiling. To be sure the Supreme Court's decision in *Whren* did not create the pretextual stop. The police have, for as long as anyone can remember, used the traffic codes to stop individuals that they believe are guilty of more serious violations. The Supreme Court merely, and unanimously, held that evidence found during a legal search is not made inadmissible because of the pretextual nature of the stop. The officers in *Whren* freely admitted that while the stop was legally justified on the basis of an observed traffic violation, they were actually suspicious that the driver may be in possession of a controlled substance. Furthermore, the Court's decision in *Whren* was not particularly surprising. For more than a decade the Court has consistently expressed its unwillingness to consider the effect an individual's race has on law enforcement decision making, a key component in the plaintiff's argument.

New Jersey is the birthplace of the racial profiling controversy. Beginning in the 1980s, minority drivers stopped along the New Jersey Turnpike (Interstate Highway 95) began to complain that they were being targeted by state troopers for drug interdiction stops. The state police routinely responded that there was no evidence that minorities are more at risk of being stopped and searched by troopers. Of course the state police were right. No stop data existed at all.

By 1990, racial profiling's "perfect storm" emerged.

First, a group of attorneys filed a series of evidence suppression hearings based principally on an alleged violation of the Equal Protection Clause. These cases were eventually merged into a single case.

Second, in an effort to evaluate the plaintiff's claims, the judge commissioned what would become the first large scale racial profiling study in the nation. This study eventually reported that African-American and Hispanic drivers are more at risk of being stopped and searched by troopers working on the New Jersey Turnpike.

Third, in a separate inquiry the court discovered credible evidence that the troopers had received a clear message (through training exercises and intelligence circulars) that drug couriers are more likely to be racial/ethnic minorities.

Fourth, several infamous stops wherein minorities were treated harshly by the police, were widely reported in the media.

Fifth, in a public statement the state police superintendent attempted to justify his trooper's behavior by suggesting that because most illegal drugs come from Central and South America, most drug couriers are Hispanic. He was fired by the governor the next day.

Sixth, the New Jersey Attorney General acknowledged that the state police were encouraged to use race-based profiles because the department's internal reward system was over-whelmingly based on drug interdiction.

Finally, the Clinton administration's Department of Justice was encouraged to use the pattern and practice statute (Section 14141) to gain control of the state police. Eventually the state police were forced to accept a highly invasive consent decree.

What We Know and Don't Know

In any controversy, it is helpful to separate what we know from what we don't know.

When adversaries focus initially on the elements of a controversy that they agree upon two important things happen.

First, the conflict becomes more manageable. The energy required to continue the controversy is focused and more productive.

Second, and more important, agreement tends to be contagious. Like in a structured sales process, wherein a series of "yeses" tends to lead to a sale, regular agreement between adversaries in a controversy tends to find common ground.

Racial profiling is more intractable because, unlike most controversies, it occurs in multiple venues (e.g., traffic enforcement, airports, investigations, etc.) and involves a very broad range of perspectives (policing practitioners, advocacy groups, scholars, etc.). In a sense racial profiling is like the evolution/intelligent design controversy that is occurring in public schools across the nation. Both sides disagree on how the Earth and the humans in it were created. The evolutionists base their argument on decades of scientific research that has withstood rigorous peer review. The intelligent design advocates base their argument in a large part on the fundamentals of their religious traditions. One side argues logic and the other faith. It is sort of like two people arguing on which flavor of ice cream is "better." Unless and until both sides agree on the framework upon which they will find a common ground, and that seems unlikely, the controversy will continue.

The racial profiling controversy involves no fewer than five adversarial groups.

1. Some racial/ethnic minorities and the groups that advocate for them are convinced that, by virtue of their minority status, they are the target of police attention.

2. The police are equally convinced that they are merely doing the job they are assigned to do.

3. Policy makers line up on both sides of the issue depending on the demands of their electorate.

4. Lawyers and judges are struggling to find precedent in this emerging area of litigation.

5. Scholars are collecting and analyzing data in an effort to find a theoretical explanation for racial profiling.

The result of this is that everybody is yelling and nobody is listening. Consider the following, rather humorous, exchange (witnessed by the author) during a public meeting wherein the results of a racial profiling study were presented (see Illustration One).

Illustration One – *Is anybody really listening?*

Professor: "The results of our study suggest that, to the extent that the population-based benchmark is accurate, Black drivers are more likely to be stopped by officers in the Bigton Police Department."

Chapter president of the NAACP: (Looking at the mayor and chief of police) "See I told you, your guys are guilty of racial profiling!"

Chief of police: "No that is not what the professor said! He just said that Black drivers are more likely to be stopped. He did not say that racial profiling is the cause."

Mayor: "Well, what else could explain the results?"

Professor: "There are several alternative explanations. For example: It could be that the police are assigned to work more in the parts of town that are principally populated by Black residents."

Chapter president: "Well isn't that racist?"

Chief: "No, we assign officers to work where they are needed and that is in high crime areas where a lot of minorities happen to live."

Chapter president: "Are you saying that Blacks are more likely to be criminals?"

City attorney: "Wait a minute, chief. Are you assigning more officers to the Black parts of town? If so, then we could be subject to an Equal Protection lawsuit."

Mayor: "We need to stop that immediately. Chief, I am ordering you to assign the same number of officers to each beat in the city! After all, everyone in the city pays taxes and deserves equal police protection."

Chapter president: "Wait a minute. You can't do that. There are parts of town that have really bad gang and drug problems. Those people need more police protection than they do in the rich parts of town."

Mayor: "Well professor, what do you suggest we do about this? Is there a solution to this problem?"

Professor: "I am sure there is, but that will require a more in depth study."

Chief: "Training, we need more training!"

One way of advancing the argument further is to look at the evidence so far. Since 1994, no fewer than 500 racial profiling studies have been conducted throughout the nation. These studies involve policing at every level (federal, state, county, local, special district, etc.), in every context (traffic enforcement, routine patrol, investigations, etc.) and from various research methods perspectives (benchmarks, data collection strategies, analytical techniques). When considered together, these studies produce a pattern of sorts. The presentation of this pattern (see Illustration Two) attempts to advance the controversy by distinguishing between what we know and what we don't know about racial profiling.

Illustration Two – *What we know and don't know about racial profiling.*

What We Know	What We Don't Know
Are minority drivers more likely to be stopped than non-minority drivers?	
When compared to benchmarks (estimates of the driving population by race and ethnicity) most studies (about 80 percent) show that minority drivers are stopped by the police in higher proportions. Some researchers conclude from this that minority drivers are more likely to be stopped by the police.	No benchmark yet exists that accurately measures the populations of individuals that are not stopped, much less the racial and ethnic proportions of these populations. In the absence of such a measure no credible researcher can conclusively state that racial and ethnic minorities are more at risk of being stopped solely because of their minority status.
If so, does this constitute racial profiling?	
Most researchers and police administrators define racial profiling as any police initiated action that primarily relies on race or ethnicity rather than the behavior of an individual or information that leads the police to a particular individual who has been identified as being, or having been, engaged in criminal activity.	Only one researcher has actually measured whether police officers are even aware of the race or ethnicity of suspects *prior* to the stop. Furthermore, no researcher has yet measured whether an officer's knowledge of an individual's race or ethnicity *actually influenced* the officer's decision to initiate a traffic stop.

Illustration Two – *Continued*

What We Know	**What We Don't Know**

Are there differences in the reason for the stop between minority and non-minority drivers?

The stated reason(s) for a traffic stop do not differ between minority and non-minority drivers.	The reason for the stop is measured very broadly so no relationships can be established between the race or ethnicity of the driver and the reason for the stop.

When stopped, are minority drivers searched more frequently than non-minority drivers?

Searches are more likely during stops involving minority drivers.	Many researchers do not consider the type of search (consent, incident to arrest, inventory, warrant, probable cause, etc.) when making this conclusion. When this factor (i.e., officer's discretion) is considered differences among racial and ethnic groups often disappear.

Do stops involving minority drivers result in more punitive responses than stops involving non-minority drivers?

Stops involving minorities result in more punitive responses from the police. For example, minority drivers are more likely than non-minority drivers to receive a citation than a warning for the same alleged violation.	In all studies the manner in which the information is collected on why drivers are stopped is overly broad and does not allow researchers to measure the severity of the alleged violation that preceded the stop.

Are minority drivers detained longer during stops than non-minority drivers?

Some studies indicate that minority drivers are detained longer than non-minority drivers.	Most researchers do not consider how other factors occurring during a stop (like arrests, searches, or time of day) affect the duration of a stop.

Illustration Two – *Continued*

What We Know	What We Don't Know

Are incidents of physical resistance/confrontation more frequent during stops involving minority drivers?

The research indicates that stops involving minority drivers are more likely to include incidents of physical confrontation or resistance. These incidents are most frequent during stops that result in arrests.	None of the research can establish the temporal order of stop events. For example, we cannot determine whether an incident of physical confrontation or resistance occurred before, during or after the decision to arrest.

Do the officers' characteristics matter?

The individual characteristics of the officers (e.g., age, gender, experience, and race) do not appear to affect their enforcement behavior.	Because very few researchers include this information, this finding is rather inconclusive.

Do officers actually know the race/ethnicity of the driver prior to the stop?

In the vast majority of stops officers are not able to accurately determine the race/ethnicity of the driver prior to the stop.	Most studies do not include a mechanism to verify the accuracy of the officers' perceptions of the drivers' race or ethnicity.

1
The Structure of Racial Profiling Research
(How do we know what we know?)

W oven into the fabric of American jurisprudence is the notion that process is more important than results. Police officers are never allowed to use the ends to justify the means. A world record contraband seizure is useless as evidence unless the police followed a Constitutionally defensible process for conducting the search.

Conducting social science research is no different. The method (or process) used by a researcher often receives more attention than the findings of the research, and justifiably so. Researchers, just like police officers, must adhere to certain procedural rules that are referred to as research methods. When a researcher violates these rules the research is considered *methodologically flawed* and its findings may be dismissed altogether. In the following, *A Case of Circular Reasoning* (see Illustration Three), a criminologist commits a serious logical thinking error. Later in this chapter you will see how some racial profiling researchers make the same mistake.

Illustration Three – *A case of circular reasoning.*

Sometimes the method used by a researcher may influence the outcome of the research. Let's say a criminologist has a theory that socially disorganized neighborhoods cause crime. This researcher may define a socially disorganized neighborhood as one wherein its residents are unable to informally handle misconduct and therefore more inclined to ask the police to intervene. The researcher may then select two neighborhoods for comparison. The neighborhood with a high number of citizen calls for service is designated as a socially disorganized neighborhood. The other neighborhood with a low number of citizen calls for service would be designated as a socially organized neighborhood. The next step would be to compare the

---

Illustration Three - *Continued*

crime rates of each neighborhood. If the researcher's theory is correct then the socially disorganized neighborhood would experience a higher rate of crime than the socially organized neighborhood. Rather than using the Uniform Crime Reports to measure crime in each neighborhood, the researcher decides that citizen calls for service is a more reliable indicator of criminal behavior. Because the socially disorganized neighborhood has a higher number of citizen calls for service the researcher concludes that socially disorganized neighborhoods cause crime.

Of course our researcher has committed a logical error. In research methods parlance we call this a tautological argument. More commonly we call this circular reasoning, or providing evidence for the validity of an assertion (in this case the researcher's theory), which assumes the validity of the assertion. Putting it another way, "I am right because I am right."

When a court rules on the admissibility of evidence, it applies one or more generally accepted procedural standards or rules. These standards are based on Constitutional law, criminal procedure codes, previous legal rulings and accepted practice. In the same way the purpose of this chapter is to subject racial profiling research to the rules and procedures commonly accepted by responsible researchers.

This chapter includes:
- A demonstration of how the definition of racial profiling can affect a racial profiling study's findings;
- An explanation of how racial profiling researchers use (sometimes inappropriately) the analytical components of a racial profiling study to determine whether a department is engaging in racial profiling;
- A discussion on the advantages and disadvantages of the commonly used methods to estimate the racial/ ethnic proportions of the population at risk of being stopped, i.e., the benchmark; and
- An examination of the three factors that affect the quality of police stop data.

Defining "Racial Profiling"

A substantial part of police work involves the application of a legal definition onto human behavior to determine whether an offense has occurred. For example, in most states to be found guilty of driving while intoxicated the prosecutor must prove that the defendant was:

1. intoxicated,
2. while operating a motor vehicle,
3. on a public highway.

Of course the driving while intoxicated statutes vary a bit from state to state, however, the process is the same. The prosecutor must prove each element of the offense beyond a reasonable doubt. If the prosecutor is able to prove that the defendant was intoxicated on a public highway but unable to prove that he was operating a motor vehicle, then the defendant is only guilty of a lesser offense, like public intoxication.

When the racial profiling controversy began during the mid-1990s, researchers, practitioners and lawmakers struggled with an acceptable definition. Some said racial profiling occurs when an individual's race influences (in any way) a police officer's decision to initiate a stop. Policing leaders argue that an officer's decision to stop a known suspect based on a description that may, among other things, include the suspect's race, should not be considered racial profiling. In fact, police officers are *supposed* to stop individuals that fit the description of a known suspect. Others argue that racial profiling occurs when individuals of one racial or ethnic group are stopped in higher proportions than they are represented among the population of drivers. More reasonable researchers argue that racial profiling occurs when a police officer makes an enforcement decision based on an assumption that individuals of a particular race are more likely guilty of a crime, such as, the possession of contraband.

Ultimately, no universally acceptable definition of racial profiling has emerged. Because researchers, practitioners and lawmakers are free to develop their own definitions there is considerable variation. Two distinct types of definitions are used. The primary distinction between them lies in the perspective from which racial profiling is measured. More importantly, the same data applied to both definitions often results in a very different outcome. Illustration Four demonstrates how a racial profiling definition can affect a study's findings.

Illustration Four – *How racial profiling definitions affect the findings of a study.*

There are two commonly used definitions of racial profiling.

Most researchers define racial profiling **conceptually**. *Among these, the most common proposes that racial profiling occurs during:*

> *...any police-initiated action that relies on the race, ethnicity, or national origin rather than the behavior of an individual or information that leads the police to a particular individual who has been identified as being, or having been, engaged in criminal activity. (Ramirez, McDevitt, & Farrell, 2000:3)*

Using this definition, to conclude racial profiling these researchers must be able to:

- *determine that police officers were aware of the race or ethnicity of individuals prior to initiating the stops, and*
- *prove that the police officers used this information as a reason for initiating a stop.*

Very few researchers are able to do this.

Among the researchers using a conceptual definition:

- *eighty percent (80%) find that minority drivers are over-represented in traffic stops, yet*
- *only twenty percent (20%) of these conclude from this evidence alone that this disparity is caused by racial profiling.*

Illustration Four - *Continued*

A small percentage of researchers define racial profiling **operationally**. *Among these, the most common definition proposes that racial profiling is:*

> *...implied as when minorities are stopped at disproportionately higher rates than they are represented within the benchmark that indicates the proportional racial representation of actual roadway users. (Lamberth, 1994).*

Using this definition, to conclude racial profiling is occurring all these researchers have to do is demonstrate that minorities are over-represented in police stops. This appears relatively easy.

Nearly all of these researchers are able to do this.

Among the researchers using an operational definition:

- *eighty percent (80%) find that minority drivers are over-represented in traffic stops, and*
- *every one of these (100%) conclude from this evidence alone that this disparity is caused by racial profiling.*

Given our inability to measure the racial proportion of the driving population, it is almost certain that a racial profiling study will find some minorities are over-represented in police stops.

So, the definition you use matters for two reasons:

- *Researchers that use a conceptual definition are seldom able to conclude racial profiling because they cannot actually measure what police officers know prior to a stop and how that knowledge affects their decision to initiate a traffic stop.*
- *Researchers that use an operational definition are nearly always able to conclude racial profiling because they only have to present evidence that minority drivers are over-represented in stops.*

The Analytical Components of Racial Profiling Research

In most racial profiling studies there are two analyses. The first attempts to determine whether one or more racial/ethnic group is over-represented in stops. The second focuses on whether one or more racial/ethnic group is treated differently during stops. With rare exception (Novak 2004; Smith and Petrocelli 2001; Withrow 2004) these analyses involve simple ratio and percentage comparisons.

How Racial Profiling Is Measured, and How It Is Not

To determine whether one or more racial/ethnic group is over-represented in stops all researchers compare the individuals (by race/ethnicity) that are stopped with the individuals (by race/ethnicity) that are available to be stopped. Normally, the race/ethnicity of the individuals stopped is reported by the police officers who complete some type of stop data form. The race/ethnicity of individuals available to be stopped is estimated by one of several methods. These estimates, generally called benchmarks, are discussed later in this chapter.

Most researches present their findings in a tabular format that compares (by racial/ethnic group) who gets stopped with who is available to be stopped. Tables 1 and 2 are typical of studies that use the residential population to estimate the driving population. Table 1 reports that Black drivers are over-represented in stops. The police report that 20.7 percent of the stops they make involve Black drivers. Using the residential population, the researcher estimates that 11.4 percent of the individuals available to be stopped are Black. As a result the researcher concludes that Blacks are over-represented and all other racial groups are under-represented in stops. In this particular study the researcher conducted a separate analysis for Hispanics. The population figures came from the United States Census Bureau wherein "Hispanic" is considered an ethnicity, separate from race. According to the Census Bureau, it is possible for an individual of any racial group to also be Hispanic (Withrow 2002).

Table 1 – *Stops by racial group (n = 37,454).*

	Percentage of population	Percentage of stops
Asian	4.0	2.9
Black	11.4	20.7
Native American	1.2	.3
White	75.2	71.1
Other Race	8.2	4.9
Not reported	-	.1
Total	**100**	**100**

Table 2 – *Stops by ethnic group (n = 37,454).*

Ethnicity	Percentage of population	Percentage of stops
Hispanic	9.6	9.2
Non Hispanic	90.4	90.3
Not reported	-	.5
Total	**100**	**100**

Of course, data is only data. What comes next is analysis and this is the source of considerable controversy. You may have noticed that the researcher in the above example used the term "over-represented." That is really all that the data reveal, *nothing more*. While some researchers may consider this over-representation evidence of racial profiling affecting Black drivers, others are justifiably more cautious. Responsible analysts understand that to establish a causal relationship between two variables (in this case being Black increases the likelihood of being stopped), *three* rules must be satisfied.

These rules are:
1. The cause must precede the effect.
2. There must be a correlation (association) between the cause and the effect.
3. All reasonable alternative explanations must be eliminated.

In this case a researcher wanting to use the above data to accuse the department of racial profiling can satisfy the first two causal rules. If *being Black* is the cause of *being stopped* then the person must be Black before he is observed by a police officer and subsequently stopped. Of course, an individual's race is literally determined at conception, well before driving age. Correlation, the second rule, means association. For two variables to be correlated means that when the cause happens the effect is either more or less likely to happen. For example, if drinking beer is a cause of weight gain then the more beer a person drinks the more weight he gains. Conversely, if exercise is the cause of weight loss then the more a person exercises the less he weighs. In our case (assuming the benchmark is an accurate estimate of the driving population) there a correlation because Black drivers appear to be more at risk of being stopped than drivers of other races. Eliminating all reasonable alternative explanations is the toughest of the three rules, and is particularly difficult in racial profiling. Indeed there are several reasonable alternative explanations for why Black drivers are over-represented in these stops (see Illustration Five).

Illustration Five – *Why racial profiling cannot be proven by a mere over-representation of minority drivers in police stops.*

- **The race of the driver is normally determined and recorded by the police officer after the decision to stop has been made.** If the race of the driver actually influenced the police officer's decision to stop then we must prove that the officer actually knew and was inappropriately motivated by the race of the driver before the decision to stop.

- **Jurisdiction wide analyses do not account for differences in patrol allocation.** Patrol resources are not spread evenly throughout a community. Patrol officers are assigned on the basis of need and usually into areas with high crime and population density. Often these areas are also populated by racial and ethnic minorities. As a result, residents of these areas are inadvertently subjected to higher levels of police observation and therefore are more likely to be stopped.

Illustration Five - *Continued*

- **There is no standard for determining how much over-representation is enough to justify an accusation of racial profiling.** Although a few researchers have tried, none have been successful in arguing that a specific level of over-representation is sufficient to prove racial profiling. If twenty-one percent of the drivers stopped by the police are Hispanic yet only twenty percent of the drivers at risk of being stopped are estimated to be Hispanic then should the police be accused of racial profiling? What if twenty-five percent of the drivers stopped by the police are Hispanic? Because there is no universally acceptable threshold a researcher's judgment on the cause of any level of over-representation of minority drivers should be considered pure speculation.

- **As a whole, some racial groups may be more likely to be observed violating the traffic laws.** It is provocative to suggest that individuals from certain racial groups are more or less likely to actually violate the traffic laws. Frankly, the evidence is inconclusive. Some studies find no difference while others find that certain racial or ethnic minorities are more likely to violate the traffic law. We do know that there is a strong correlation between race/ethnicity and socio-economic class. Racial and ethnic minorities tend to be economically less advantaged. Social class may also play a significant role in the types of crime an individual commits. Individuals from lower socio-economic class tend to commit a higher proportion of street crimes and are therefore more likely to be observed by patrol officers.

The Promise and Peril of Post-Stop Analyses

Post-stop analyses focus on what happens to drivers after they are stopped. Primarily these analyses attempt to determine whether certain racial/ethnic minorities are treated differently during stops. Beyond this, these analyses are quite useful for evaluating the efficiency and effectiveness of routine patrol operations. In fact, the ultimate contribution of racial profiling research may eventually be in what it teaches us about how patrol officers actually work.

Post-stop analyses do not use driving population benchmarks and are therefore not susceptible to the error associated with these estimates. The baseline population upon which these analyses are conducted is actually established by the police stop data. Here again, with rare exception (Novak 2004, Smith and Petrocelli 2001, Withrow 2004), these analyses involve simple ratio and percentage comparisons (see Illustration Six).

Illustration Six – *Common post-stop analysis questions.*

- Are members of all racial/ethnic groups stopped for essentially the same reasons or types of violations?
- During a stop are individuals of certain racial/ethnic groups more or less likely to be searched?
- Are members of certain racial/ethnic groups more likely to be arrested?
- Are members of certain racial/ethnic groups more likely to be issued a citation instead of a warning?
- Are stops involving certain racial/ethnic groups more likely to last longer?
- Do officers tend to request additional help (i.e., backup) when they stop individuals of certain racial/ethnic groups?
- Are stops involving certain racial/ethnic groups more likely to involve incidents of physical resistance or confrontation?

The statistical comparisons used in most post-stop analyses are often misinterpreted unless the analyst has a well-rounded knowledge of police systems and practices. A solid understanding of the context from which the statistics come is essential. For example, an analyst may find that stops involving Hispanic drivers tend to last longer than stops involving drivers of other racial/ethnic groups. He may conclude from this that Hispanic drivers are subjected to higher levels of police interrogation, scrutiny or are hassled by the police. A more plausible explanation should be considered. If a sizeable proportion of the community's Hispanic population is Spanish speaking then longer duration stops may be the result of a language barrier.

Sometimes seemingly unrelated factors can confound the analyst's findings. For example, a researcher may find that officers tend to request additional assistance during stops involving Black drivers. This may appear as if the police are "ganging up" on Black drivers. However, the analyst may overlook the fact that in this particular community Black residents (and drivers) may be over-represented in high crime areas. Routine patrol operations are much different in high crime areas and often involve officers working in closely connected teams. In addition, in high crime areas a higher proportion of stops involve searches, and therefore require additional assistance.

No racial profiling researcher has successfully documented how the order of events affects the outcome of a stop. For example, a few researchers have found that stops involving Black drivers are more likely to include incidents of physical resistance or confrontation. Unfortunately, these researchers cannot determine what preceded these incidents. Did the physical confrontation occur after the police searched the vehicle, found contraband and arrested the driver? Or, did the physical confrontation occur first, thereby justifying an arrest?

Racial profiling researchers have a habit of asking the wrong question. For example, many researchers ask whether members of all racial/ethnic groups are stopped for essentially the same reasons or type of violation? Not a bad question, but what they really want to know is whether racial/ethnic minorities are stopped for less severe violations of the law? If on the average speeding Black drivers are stopped at five miles over the limit while speeding White drivers are stopped at ten miles over the limit then the analyst is likely justified in finding that Black drivers are held to a stricter standard. In other words, Black drivers don't have to do as much as White drivers to receive the attention of the police. Unfortunately, most racial profiling researchers do not collect data in sufficient detail to properly assess these nuances. Most stop data include only four to six possible reasons for the stop. Nearly always "traffic violation" is included as a choice. However, a traffic violation could be as serious as driving five miles over the speed limit on a rural interstate highway or as serious as five miles over the speed limit in an occupied school zone. Most stop data sets do not contain sufficient information to determine whether racial/ethnic minorities are more likely to be stopped for less severe violations of the law.

The two post-stop analyses that receive the most attention involve searches and enforcement decisions. These are among the most discretionary decisions made by police officers and justifiably should receive most of our attention. Here again, common sense and a good working knowledge of police patrol operations is essential.

Searches are an important part of police work and often the most controversial aspect of a racial profiling study. Most researchers use simple ratio comparisons to determine whether individuals from certain racial/ethnic groups are more likely to be subjected to a search. Table 3 is typical of this type of analysis. The "benchmark" in this case is the percentage of individuals actually stopped by race. These data indicate that Black drivers, when stopped, are more likely to be searched.

Table 3 – *Percentage of individuals searched by race.*

Race	Percentage of stops	Percentage of searches
Asian	2.9	1.6
Black	20.7	37.2
Native American	.3	0
White	71.1	57.2
Other Race	4.9	3.0
Not reported	.1	1.0
Total	100	100

The underlying message is that Black drivers are searched because they are Black. More responsible analysts familiar with routine police operations know that not all searches are created equal. The key issue here is not whether somebody was searched. The most important concern is whether somebody was searched unjustly or arbitrarily. Only when the various types of searches are analyzed separately can we determine whether the police overstepped their discretionary authority (see Table 4).

Table 4 – *Percentage of individuals searched by race and type of search.*

Race	% of stops	% of all searches	% inventory searches	% searches incident to arrest	% probable cause/ Warrant searches	% plain view searches	% consent searches
Asian	2.9	1.6	1.8	2.0	2.0	2.4	3.2
Black	20.7	37.2	47.8	48.1	22.1	22.0	16.3
Native American	.3	0	1.1	1.0	.5	.4	.5
White	71.1	57.2	46.6	46.1	70.4	70.1	77.1
Other Race	4.9	3.0	2.1	2.3	4.8	5.0	2.6
Not reported	.1	1.0	.6	.5	.2	.1	.3
Total	100	100	100	100	100	100	100

When these searches are analyzed with respect to their justification, an alternative finding emerges. Inventory searches and searches incident to arrest are non-discretionary. In many cases the police are required by law or policy to search an individual or vehicle following an arrest or vehicle impoundment. In this particular case Black drivers are more likely to be the subject of inventory and incident to arrest searches because they are also more likely to be arrested. While the effect race plays on the likelihood of an arrest is within itself an important consideration, the factors affecting the probability of an arrest should be considered separately from the analysis of searches, at least initially. Probable cause and warrant-based searches are a little more discretionary yet they assume the officer is able to articulate a valid reason for conducting a search. Plain view searches are more discretionary, however, they assume that officers observed evidence of a crime in plain sight and were therefore justified in conducting a search. It is important to notice (see Table 4) that the percentage of individuals by race that were subjected to a probable cause, warrant-based and plain view search are very close to the overall percentages of individuals stopped. This should be interpreted to mean that the race of the driver appears to have no influence on an officer's decision to conduct a probable cause and warrant-based search or to observe contraband in plain view.

Because of their discretionary nature, consent searches deserve special attention. These particular data indicate that while Black drivers represent 20.7 percent of all stops, only 16.3 percent of all consent searches involve Black drivers. On the other hand, Whites represent 71.1 percent of all stops and 77.1 percent of all consent searches. One could conclude from this that when stopped White drivers are more likely to be subjected to a consent search.

Some racial profiling researchers attempt to analyze searches with contraband seizures. Typically they compare the search hit rates between racial/ethnic groups. For example, the data in Table 5 suggest that consent searches involving White drivers are more likely to result in a contraband seizure. Conversely, these data suggest that consent searches involving Black drivers are less likely to result in contraband seizures. Of course the implication is that the police should search White drivers more than Black drivers. This conclusion is incorrect because it does not recognize two important realities in routine police operations. Searches are never justified on the basis of whether or not contraband is seized. Searches are justified on the basis of whether the police followed a Constitutionally permissible process while conducting the search. Furthermore, every search is an independent event driven by an individual's behavior and/or the presence of evidence within the context of a stop. A police officer's decision to initiate a search should be influenced by the evidence at hand and not a probability that is artificially based on the race of the driver. In fact, *not* searching is just as much racial profiling as searching if the decision not to search is based on the race of the driver.

Table 5 – *Search hit rates by racial/ethnic group.*

Race	Percentage of stops	Percentage consent searches	Percentage producing contraband
Asian	2.9	3.2	3.0
Black	20.7	16.3	9.2
Native American	.3	.5	.5
White	71.1	77.1	82.0
Other Race	4.9	2.6	5.0
Not reported	.1	.3	.3
Total	100	100	100

Stop outcome analyses attempt to determine whether a driver's race/ethnicity affects a police officer's decision to arrest, cite or warn pursuant to an observed violation. Here again, these analyses are hampered by a lack of precision in how the reason for the stop is measured. The punitiveness of the officer's response to a law violation (ranging from verbal warning – written warning – citation – arrest) should be related to the severity of the driver's behavior. An individual observed speeding ten miles over the limit might be given a warning on a rural interstate highway, but a citation in an occupied school zone. Unfortunately, when the reason for the stop is recorded in both of these cases it may be broadly categorized as a "traffic violation." This lack of measurement precision prohibits analysts from evaluating the appropriateness of a stop's disposition because no relationship can be established between the severity, flagrance or dangerousness of the driver's behavior and the punitiveness of the officer's response. Ideally, the analysis should be able to determine whether an individual is more likely to receive a more formal sanction (e.g., a citation instead of a warning) pursuant to a more serious violation of the law.

The Denominator Problem
(measuring who does not get stopped)

From a research methods perspective, measuring who does not get stopped is the most difficult and controversial aspect of racial profiling research. In a way it is like measuring who does not commit a crime, or better yet, who commits a crime that nobody knows about. In spite of fifteen years of active   research and litigation, no universally accepted method for estimating the population of individuals at risk of being stopped has emerged.

While there is considerable variation within each of the following categories, the benchmarks used by researchers are primarily based on:
1. residential populations,
2. field observations, or
3. accident records

How Benchmarks Are Developed

Population-based benchmarks are by far the most commonly used. Most are based on the racial/ethnic proportions within the residential population as reported or estimated by the United States Bureau of the Census or other authoritative sources. If the police stop data contain information on all individuals (including juveniles) who may come in contact with the police, then the researcher should use the entire population of the community (Withrow 2002, 2003). Some researchers only use the estimated population of licensed drivers (Smith and Petrocelli 2001). And a few researchers adjust the population using weighting factors like vehicle ownership (Rojek, Rosenfeld and Decker 2004) or population centers within a metropolitan area (Novak 2004).

Field observation-based benchmarks are developed by systematically observing drivers in traffic at and during randomly selected locations and times. Most studies attempt to record the race, ethnicity, gender and age of the observed drivers (Police Foundation 2003). In addition, some researchers attempt to identify the drivers (also by race/ ethnicity, age and gender) who are observed violating the traffic law, and therefore more likely to be stopped (Lamberth 1994). One research team even used digital cameras and speed detection technology to record images of drivers and their speed (Lange, Blackman and Johnson 2001). Field observation benchmarks are then compared to the police stop data that is collected at or near where the benchmarks are collected.

Accident records are used extensively by traffic engineers and automobile insurance companies to develop risk factors among drivers (Alpert, Smith and Dunham 2003). This is why our teenage sons pay high automobile insurance rates. In racial profiling research the focus is on the not-at-fault drivers in two vehicle accidents. The Washington State Patrol (2001) introduced this technique to the racial profiling research agenda. The logic of this benchmarking strategy is based on two factors. First, from the not-at-fault drivers' perspectives an accident is a random event. An appropriate sample of these events provides insight into the race, ethnicity, gender and age of the driving population. Second, individuals who drive more often are more at risk of being involved in an accident. They are also more at risk of being observed by a police officer. So accident records based on benchmarks naturally include a weighting factor for driving frequency.

Benchmarks and Their Measurement Error

No single benchmarking strategy can be applied to every research setting. Population-based benchmarks are not effective in rural traffic situations (e.g., interstate highways) where a stable residential population does not exist. Field observation-based benchmarks are less reliable in low-light (e.g., nighttime), high speed and heavy traffic settings. Accident records-based benchmarks are often hampered by a lack of information (e.g., race, ethnicity, age, gender) on not-at-fault drivers and an inability to accurately determine which driver is truly not-at-fault. The relative advantages and disadvantages of these commonly used benchmarking strategies are summarized in Illustration Seven.

Illustration Seven – *Relative advantages and disadvantages of commonly used benchmarking strategies in racial profiling research.*

Strategy	Advantages	Disadvantages
Population	• Readily available and inexpensive. • Can be applied to an entire jurisdiction or a single beat or neighborhood. • Can be used to evaluate non-traffic contacts between the police and juveniles.	• Does not include the transient population – people who drive but do not live in a community. • Does not account for differential exposure to police observation based on where people live, where the police are assigned and how much people drive. • The historic underreporting of some racial/ethnic minorities may skew the population estimates.

Strategy	Advantages	Disadvantages
Illustration Seven - *Continued*		
Field observations	• Accounts for the transient population – people who drive but do not live in a community. • Accounts for differential exposure to police observation based on where people live, where the police are assigned and how much people drive. • Can be used in areas that do not have a stable residential population. • Can distinguish between violator and non-violator populations.	• Very expensive and time consuming to collect. • Potentially unreliable and invalid in low light, high volume an high speed locations. • Limits analysis to the observation site. • Difficult to associate the benchmark with a relevant portion of the police stop data because stops may not occur where the violations are observed and vice versa.
Accident records	• Readily available and inexpensive in most jurisdictions. • Accounts for the transient population – people who drive but do not live in a community. • Accounts for differential exposure to police observation based on where people live, where the police are assigned and how much people drive. • Can be applied to an entire jurisdiction or a single beat or neighborhood. • Can be applied to nearly every research context.	• There are no empirical studies that have validated the accuracy of this estimate. • In many jurisdictions accident records do not include the race/ethnicity of the not-at-fault driver. • It is difficult to determine which driver is truly not-at-fault.

Stop Data (measuring who gets stopped)

Prior to 1995 had anybody asked a police chief about the percentage of stops made by the officers in his department involving Black drivers, it is likely that he could only guess. Prior to the racial profiling controversy, police administrators actually knew very little about how their officers worked, comparatively speaking. Today thanks to the police stop data collected for racial profiling research we know a great deal about how officers work and make decisions. An extensive discussion on how to improve the quality of police stop data occurs in a later chapter. For the purposes of this chapter the focus below is on three important data collection concepts.

Accuracy

The accuracy of police stop data is a common concern among racial profiling researchers. Some researchers and commentators question the truthfulness of the police based on a notion that the police, motivated by a fear of retribution, will lie when reporting the race/ethnicity of the drivers they stop. Given that most racial profiling studies find racial and ethnic minorities are over-represented in police stops, if the police are lying, they are not doing a very good job of it. Fact is, out of the hundreds of racial profiling studies done during the past fifteen years, only one researcher (Lamberth 1994) found any evidence of police misconduct.

In his New Jersey Turnpike Study, Lamberth identified two types of police misconduct in stop data collection.

Ghosting – When the police report that minority drivers are White so as to reduce the proportion of minority drivers actually stopped.

Balancing – When the police amend their stop reporting forms so that the racial/ethnic proportions of individuals stopped closely approximates that of the benchmark.

One of the most common threats to the accuracy of police stop data is the misinterpretation of a driver's race or ethnicity. While an individual's race may appear obvious, given the increasing proportion of multiracial individuals within the general population, the probability of an officer misinterpreting a driver's race or ethnicity is increasing. Some researchers have suggested that officers should simply ask. Unfortunately, such a request might insult the driver or taint the contact with an air of racial tension (Fridell et al. 2001). Several tips for improving the accuracy of police stop data are offered in a later chapter.

Completeness

Incomplete data sets threaten the viability of racial profiling research. Information from police/citizen contacts as diverse as field interviews, pedestrian stops, traffic stops resulting in verbal or written warnings, citations and arrests are normally captured in the police stop data sets used in racial profiling research. Unfortunately, the completeness of a stop data set is difficult to assess because a single repository of police activity measures seldom exists. Citations and written warnings may be recorded in one database while field interviews are catalogued in another. Contacts resulting in verbal warnings may not be recorded at all. As will be discussed in a later chapter, often the best way to insure the completeness of police stop data is to make the racial profiling data collection process as seamless as possible within the department's overall productivity measures.

Reactivity

Reactivity, a threat to the validity of data, happens when research subjects alter their behavior because they are aware that they are being studied or measured. This is a particularly important consideration in police stop data collection because racial profiling research projects seldom happen without substantial public discussion. Police officers may justifiably be apprehensive about collecting the very data that may be used against them. As will be discussed in a later chapter, the best way to mitigate this is to assure officers that their personal information will not be disclosed publically.

2

How Racial Profiling Data Is (*Or Should Be*) Collected and Consumed

In the history of American policing no issue has caused more data collection than the racial profiling controversy. Even the grant largesse of the Law Enforcement Assistance Administration in the late 1960s, the advent of the community/problem oriented policing paradigms in the late 1980s, and the current emphasis on intelligence-led policing have not caused police departments to collect such detailed data on their routine enforcement programs, as has the racial profiling controversy. To date more than 500 policing agencies at all levels either have collected or are currently collecting data to be used specifically for a racial profiling study. In addition, police departments in no fewer than twenty-seven states are required by statute to routinely collect information on the stops they make.

The racial profiling controversy is a statistician's dream. The analytical possibilities are seemingly endless. Statistics are only numbers and cannot possibly capture the contextual complexity of the police function. Every traffic stop is preceded by a police officer's decision and these decisions are influenced by dozens of factors most of which cannot be measured with numerical accuracy. Within each traffic stop a police officer makes dozens of decisions that are motivated by numerous factors not the least of which are the driver's behavior and responses to the officer's inquiries. Borrowing a phrase from my officer street survival colleagues – *there is no such thing as a routine traffic stop.*

The purpose of this chapter is to provide policing leaders with guidance on how racial profiling data should be collected, analyzed and consumed. The overall objective of any data collection system, and this one particularly, is seamlessness. Police departments already collect large volumes of data. So, is it any wonder that policing leaders are resistant to collecting more, especially the very data that may result in their public ridicule? The key to success is to find a way to routinely, comprehensively and unobtrusively document police/citizen contacts. Next, this chapter includes a brief discussion on how racial profiling data should be analyzed. The American humorist Mark Twain is credited with saying, "There are lies, damned lies and statistics." Statistics, admittedly, is not the most popular course on campus. It is, however, important to have a general understanding of how analysis is conducted in order to be a more critical consumer of the research. Following this a potential solution is proposed that has demonstrated a capacity to overcome many of the common data collection obstacles in racial profiling research. Finally, this chapter concludes with an argument for enlisting the assistance of a competent research partner. Knowing how to *crunch the numbers* is one thing. Understanding what the numbers mean requires an individual who is skilled in statistical analysis and knowledgeable about routine police operations.

Two Key Data Collection Concepts

Data collection is, or should be, a very methodical process. Ultimately, the viability of a research study depends on the quality of the data it collects. Because data collection is so expensive and time consuming, it is important to get it right. Fortunately, there are some effective rules that, if followed, will produce quality data.

Variables and Attributes
Variables and their attributes are the foundation of effective data collection. A variable is anything that varies. Race, age, weight, income, etc., are all variables because they may vary from person to person. Most variables have both a direct and an indirect meaning. For example, income can be defined directly by the number of dollars one earns in a year. Income can also be used indirectly to define poverty or socio-economic status.

Attributes are the categories associated with a variable. Some variables have a limited number of attributes. For example, the variable gender has two attributes – male and female. Other variables have a nearly unlimited number of attributes. Income can range from zero to billions of dollars and even beyond.

Effective variables and attributes have three qualities – *precise meaning*, *mutual exclusivity* and *exhaustiveness*. Illustration Eight proposes a method for insuring the variable describing an individual's race can meet these three criteria.

Illustration Eight – *Qualities of effective variables and attributes.*

Beginning variable and attributes

Variable	Attributes
Race	Caucasian/White African-American/Black

Quality	Definition	What if problem
Precise meaning	The ability of a variable to clearly describe a single feature.	A police officer describes Sam, an individual of Middle Eastern heritage, as Caucasian. Sam describes himself as African-American. The officer objects. Sam says he is an American citizen originally from Egypt and then reminds the officer that Egypt is in Africa.
Mutual exclusivity	The ability of a set of attributes to classify an individual into one, and only one, category.	A police officer describes Conchita, a native of Barbados, as African-American because her skin is black. Conchita correctly describes herself as Caucasian/Hispanic. The officer, knowing that stops involving Hispanics are an important issue in his department, can't decide whether to describe Conchita as Caucasian (which she technically is, but not white skinned) or African-American (which she is not, but is black skinned).
Exhaustiveness	The ability of a set of attributes to classify all, or almost all, individuals.	A police officer describes Wan Li, a Chinese-American as Caucasian. Wan Li describes himself as Asian. Wan Li does not fit in either of the available categories.

Illustration Eight - *Continued*

Solution: Because technical accuracy in classifying a driver's race is not as important as an officer's perception of the individual's race, skin color (objectively visible by the officer) is likely a more important variable than race. In most situations, 'Hispanic' is considered an ethnicity, independent of race. It is possible for a person to be both black skinned and Hispanic. It is therefore necessary to separate race and ethnicity into two variables. The actual attributes used may vary between jurisdictions depending on the racial/ethnic composition of the driving population. Of course it is not practical to include all possible combinations of races and ethnicities into a stop form. As a rule of thumb an 'other' category can be used for up to five percent of the population that do not fit into one of the major categories. Finally, it is also important for the race/ethnicity categories in the police stop data to match those in the benchmark. The following meet the three qualities of effective variables and attributes.

Improved variables and attributes

Variable	Attributes
Race/Skin color	White
	Black
	Native-American
	Asian
	Other
Ethnicity	Hispanic
	Non-Hispanic

Level of Measurement

The level of measurement used for a variable determines how the variable is measured and ultimately analyzed. There are four levels of measurement. Each level has its own distinct characteristic (see Illustration Nine).

Nominal variables differentiate between individuals by merely naming them. Race is a nominal variable whose attributes (e.g., Black, Caucasian, Asian, Native-American, etc.) cannot be arranged in a logical order.

Ordinal variables also name things but can be arranged in a logical order. The winner of an Olympic track event receives a gold medal, while the second and third place finishers receive silver and bronze medals, respectively. Gold, silver and bronze are names we associate with the first, second and third place finishers. These names can be also arranged in a logical order – gold, silver, bronze or bronze, silver and gold. Unfortunately the differences between each of these may vary. The difference between the gold and silver medal winners may be 3.2 seconds, while the difference between the silver and bronze medal winners may be 4.3 seconds.

Interval variables can be arranged in a logical order and the differences between these are the same. Weight is an interval level measure. The difference between a 200-pound person and a 201-pound person (one pound) is the same as the difference between a 250-pound person and a 251-pound person. Interval measured variables can also be arranged in a logical order. For example, individuals in a data set can be arranged from heaviest to lightest or lightest to heaviest. Interval measured variables can also be converted to nominal level variables. The analyst can specify individuals by weight into two or more nominal categories – light weight, welter weight, heavy weight, etc.

Ratio variables have the same qualities as interval variables and have an absolute zero level. Temperature is a ratio variable. Here again, ratio variables can be converted into a lower level of measurement by the analyst. Daily high temperatures can be arranged in a logical order from hottest to coldest or coldest to hottest. The analyst can also classify temperatures into two or more nominal categories – hot, warm, tepid, cool, cold, etc.

Illustration Nine – *Levels of measurement.*

Level	Name	Rank order	Equal distance	Absolute zero	Example	Measure of central tendency
Nominal	X				Race	Mode
Ordinal	X	X			Olympic race results (gold, silver, bronze)	Mode Median
Interval	X	X	X		Weight	Mode Median Mean
Ratio	X	X	X	X	Temperature	Mode Median Mean

Ideally, variables should at least be measured at the interval or ratio level. These are the most precise and analytically flexible levels of measurement. It is always possible to convert a variable from a higher level to a lower level of measurement (i.e., ratio→interval→ordinal→nominal), however, it is never possible to convert a variable from a lower level to a higher level of measurement (e.g., nominal→ordinal→interval→ratio). Illustration Ten shows how a simple change in how a variable is measured can produce more informative results. For all practical purposes, internal and ratio variables are analyzed the same way.

Illustration Ten – *How a minor change in how a variable is measured can make the analysis more informative.*

The relationship between the reason for a stop and the outcome of a stop is a critical issue in racial profiling research. Ideally, the relationship between these two variables should be positive, meaning the more serious the violation the more punitive the outcome. Individuals stopped for more serious violations are more likely to be arrested than individuals who are stopped for minor violations. Critics of the police allege that minorities are more likely to be arrested or cited than non-minorities regardless of the seriousness of the offense.

To determine the relationship between these two variables (i.e., reason for the stop and results of the stop) they should be collected at either the interval or ratio level. Unfortunately, in most racial profiling studies the attributes for these variables are collected at the nominal level and cannot be arranged in a logical order of increasing severity.

Typical attributes in racial profiling research for

Reason for the stop	**Results of the stop**
● Traffic violation	● Arrest
● Equipment violation	● Citation
● Probable cause	● Warning
● Suspicious circumstances	● Police case generated
● DUI/DL checklane	● No action
● Service rendered	

The reason for the stop variable is particularly problematic. There is a lot of variation within each of this variable's attributes. For example, a traffic violation could be as serious as speeding 10 mph over the limit in a busy school zone or as minor as 5 miles per hour over the limit on a rural interstate highway. Furthermore, these attributes cannot be arranged in any logical order. The issue here is not the actual violation. It is the severity of the violation that likely determines the harshness of the outcome. Replacing this variable with a scale indicating the relative severity of the violation, ranging from 1 (low severity) to 10 (high severity), to be completed by the officer initiating the stop would solve this problem.

Reformatting the attributes for the results of the stop variable is not so problematic. There is a logical order of harshness within these attributes with no action being the least to an arrest being the most punitive.

Improved attributes in racial profiling research for:

Severity of the observed violation that initiated the stop	Results of the stop
Officer indicates the severity on a scale ranging from 1 (low severity) to 10 (high severity)	● Arrest ● Citation ● Written warning ● Verbal warning ● No action taken

Now the relationship between these variables can be analyzed using a simple Pearson r statistic to determine if the severity of the observed violation initiating the stop affects the outcome of the stop. Furthermore, more complicated statistical models could be used to better assess the influence of race on the outcome of the stop while also considering the severity of the observed offense.

Eventually, the data you collect will be analyzed. The availability and precision of statistical techniques that can be used by the analyst increase with the level of measurement. For example, if the data is collected at the nominal level, the only measure of central tendency (commonly called an average) available is the mode, or the most frequently occurring attribute. If the data is collected at the ordinal level, the analyst can use the median (the middle value) and the mode. If the data are collected at either the interval or ratio levels, the analyst can use the mean (what most people consider the average), the median and the mode. A more detailed discussion on analytical strategies appears later in this chapter.

Document Stops, Routinely

Resistance to racial profiling data collection is understandable. Police departments have historically collected vast amounts of data and with the advent of various information-hungry programs like COMPSTAT and intelligence-led policing they will likely be asked to collect more. The resistance to collecting racial profiling data is particularly acute because this information is often used to malign the department's public image.

Many police officers object to collecting racial profiling data because of the inference that comes with it. Racial profiling studies do not occur in a vacuum. They are public events that are often precipitated *and* followed by accusations of racism. In the words of an anonymous police chief, "Why should we go through the expense and trouble of collecting data that will only be used by politicians who want to trash us and plaintiffs who want to sue us?"

Racial profiling studies produce statistics and most people don't trust statistical analysis. Statistics seldom produce definitive answers and statisticians live in a grey world dominated by inference, probabilities and levels of acceptable error. For example, "Based on the available data, it appears African-American drivers are more likely to be stopped than Caucasian drivers" is a common phrase used by racial profiling researchers. Of course, the inference is that the police are targeting African-American drivers *because* they are African-American. Racial profiling studies seldom attempt to "go behind the numbers" and determine why African-

American drivers are over-represented in stops. Frustration with a racial profiling study's lack of insight led a patrol captain to quip, "These studies never solve a damn thing. They never convince anybody of anything."

There are, however, considerable advantages to collecting data on police stops. It is very likely that a decade from now the value of the racial profiling studies conducted today will lie in what they teach us about how patrol officers work. Prior to the racial profiling controversy few police administrators could have responded accurately to even the most rudimentary questions about police patrol operations. Most could only guess when asked how long the average stop lasts or what percentage of consent searches result in a contraband seizure.

Comprehensive data collections provide administrators with important insights into the effectiveness and efficiency of their officers. Stop studies may also reveal important training deficiencies. For example, after learning that only two percent of all consent searches result in a contraband seizure a police administrator may be convinced that his officers need additional interdiction training.

Racial profiling studies provide police departments with a platform upon which to improve their relationships with racial/ethnic minority communities. Voluntarily conducting a racial profiling study conveys a department's commitment to unbiased policing and the value of equal protection. Formal racial profiling inquiries involving community stakeholders provide a broad range of citizens the opportunity to learn how their police department operates. Even the most vocal critics of the police are often satiated when they learn the complexity of the police function.

Finally, the most convincing argument for routinely collecting data on police stops may lie in our experience with in-car video. When in-car video systems were first developed the majority of police officers refused to use them, citing concerns about privacy and an increased risk of civil liability. Eventually we learned that video (now digital) recordings of police stops are more likely to support a police officer's version of what happened during the stop. Today, police officers routinely object when assigned a car without an operable camera. One reason racial profiling studies fail to settle arguments may be that we don't document enough.

Police decision making is highly contextual in that the events surrounding each stop influence both the decision to stop as well as all other decisions made during the stop. If we don't collect enough data to accurately describe the context of each stop then it is not likely we will be able to justify a police officer's decisions prior to and during a stop.

The Mechanics of Data Collection

"It's not what you know, it is how you know it," is a common phrase used by social science researchers. More attention is given to the method of social science research than the results because social phenomena and human behavior are more difficult to measure. In the 'hard' sciences measurement is precise, standardized and universally accepted. Chemist measure the properties of a substance at the molecular level. Physicists measure the velocity of a moving object in miles, or even seconds, per hour. Ecologists measure the impurities in water in parts per million. Social scientists are not so fortunate. How does one accurately measure a suspect's demeanor, a police officer's motivation for initiating a stop or the factors that lead an officer to request a consent search.

Ultimately, the value of any social science research, including racial profiling research, is determined by the strength of its method. If the method is flawed then the results of the research are questionable. The following sections provide a brief overview of some of the most important factors that should be considered when collecting racial profiling related police stop data. This discussion is limited to the collection of police stop data. Issues relating to the collection of a benchmark, arguably a critical issue in racial profiling research, are discussed in Chapter One.

Writing Questions

Deciding what you want to learn is the first step of every research project. This may seem obvious, but a lack of specificity and focus are the most common causes of a research project's failure. Illustration Eleven includes a list of the most common questions asked in racial profiling research.

Illustration Eleven – *Commonly asked questions in racial profiling research.*

1. Are racial and ethnic minorities stopped more frequently than non-minority citizens?
2. Are there differences in the reasons for stops with respect to the race or ethnicity of the driver?
3. Are racial and ethnic minorities searched more frequently than non-minorities?
4. Does the disposition of the stop differ with respect to the race or ethnicity of the individual stopped?
5. Are racial and ethnic minorities detained longer during a stop than non-minorities?
6. Are incidents of physical resistance or confrontation more frequent during stops involving racial or ethnic minorities?
7. What effect does officer characteristics have on the representation of minorities in traffic stops?

These are good research questions, but most are overly broad and largely unresponsive to the issues that matter most to the racial profiling controversy. For example, not all searches (see Question #3 above) are created equal. Some searches (e.g., inventory, incident to arrest) are required by statute or policy. Some (e.g., plain view, probable cause) are based on some level of proof that an offense has been or is being committed. Other searches (e.g., consent) are based on an officer's hunch. The critical question in a racial profiling inquiry is whether police officers are inappropriately influenced by a driver's race/ethnicity when conducting a discretionary (i.e., consent) search. In Illustration Twelve the commonly asked racial profiling questions are rewritten to be more specific or relevant to the salient issues in the racial profiling controversy. This of course is only a general list. Research questions should be tailored to address the specific concerns of each study or jurisdiction. The reader will also note that the process of writing more specific or relevant questions provides some guidance on the variables that need to be collected within the stop data. Finally, researchers should resist the urge to "throw in a few more questions." Data collection is expensive and time consuming. Every minute a police officer uses to fill out a stop form is a minute not devoted to routine patrol or more pressing crime control activities. Collectively, these minutes add up and can seriously reduce the availability of patrol resources.

Illustration Twelve – *More specific and relevant racial profiling study questions.*

Original Questions	More Specific/Relevant Questions
Are racial and ethnic minorities stopped more frequently than non-minority citizens?	Considering the racial/ethnic proportions within the population of traffic law violators and how and where officers are assigned to work, what racial/ethnic group(s) are more likely to be stopped?
Are there differences in the reasons for stops with respect to the race or ethnicity of the driver?	Are drivers of some racial/ethnic groups more likely to be stopped for less serious violations?
Are racial and ethnic minorities searched more frequently than non-minorities?	What types of searches do our officers conduct? Within the moderately discretionary (plain view, probable cause) and highly discretionary (consent) search categories are some racial/ethnic groups over-represented when compared to their representation among all drivers stopped? Do factors relating to the stop (location, crime rate, time of day, number of occupants, etc.) affect the frequency of consent searches?
Does the disposition of the stop differ with respect to the race or ethnicity of the individual stopped?	When all factors affecting the outcome of a stop are considered (seriousness of the offense, enforcement context of the stop, time of day, violator's demeanor, etc.), are drivers of certain racial/ethnic groups more likely to either be arrested, cited, warned in writing, or verbally warned?
Are racial and ethnic minorities detained longer during a stop than non-minorities?	When all factors affecting the duration of a traffic stop are considered (arrests, search, communications issues, time of day, number of occupants, etc.), do stops involving drivers of certain racial/ethnic groups last longer?
Are incidents of physical resistance or confrontation more frequent during stops involving racial or ethnic minorities?	When, during the traffic stop (e.g., before or after the decision to arrest), do incidents of physical resistance or confrontation tend to happen? How does the department distinguish between "physical resistance" and "confrontation"? When contextual factors relating to the stop are considered (time of day, crime rate, number of occupants, age of driver, etc.), are drivers of certain racial/ethnic groups more likely to be involved in incidents of physical resistance or confrontation with the police?
What effect does officer characteristics have on the representation of minorities in traffic stops?	Does an officer's race/ethnicity, age, level of experience, gender, etc., affect the racial/proportion of drivers stopped by the officer?

Data Collection Alternatives

The method used to actually collect police stop data is an important consideration. Three formats are commonly used, however, technology may provide additional methods in the future. Each have their own advantages and disadvantages and none of them are universally feasible (see Illustration Thirteen). In other words, the best method to collect stop depends on the data collection infrastructure and resources available to the department.

Illustration Thirteen – *Advantages/disadvantages of the various stop data collection methods.*

Method	Advantages	Disadvantages
Machine readable paper forms (Bubble forms)	Relatively inexpensive Do not require major software changes to a department's information system	Take up space in patrol cars and central filing systems Distribution may be problematic. Process of converting the data on them to electronic media may introduce some error. No real-time integrity checks Lag time between when data are recorded (by the police) and available for analysis.
Portable electronic devices (MDTs, PDAs, laptops)	Easier to complete if menu driven Real time integrity checks are possible No form distribution problems	May require considerable software changes to a department's information system. May need to procure additional equipment. Additional expenses associated with officer training and maintenance.
Existing data from current information systems (CAD, Dispatch systems)	Lack of potential reactivity No addition officer time necessary to collect data	Quite rare to find acceptable level of detail to support a racial profiling inquiry. Current information systems are normally not comprehensive enough to support a rigorous racial profiling inquiry.

To the extent possible, racial profiling data collection should be merged into the data collection systems (e.g., citation, warning, field interview forms, etc) that are already familiar to the officers. This rule may be relaxed if the data collection period is too brief (one year or less) to justify a comprehensive revision of the department's commonly used forms. **Here are some tips for making data collection routine and productive.**

Data collection should be nearly free of human intervention. Data is generally more accurate at the point where it is created, i.e., when the officer completes the stop record immediately following the stop. Human intervention subsequent to the point where the information is captured by the patrol officer (e.g., data entry) increases the potential for error. This can be completely avoided with Mobile Display Terminal (MDT) based data collection systems or at least greatly reduced by the use of machine readable forms.

Data collection systems should include automatic edit protocols. Edit protocols, normally embedded into an electronic data based design, identify obvious mistakes and logical errors so they can be rejected and then corrected before resubmission. For example, it is not possible for a pedestrian to be stopped for a speeding violation. Edit protocols would identify this as a mistake and resubmit the record to the officer for correction prior to allowing it to become a permanent part of the data set.

Data collection systems should be able to assess the accuracy of the data set. Assessing accuracy may require connecting stop data reports with specific individuals and/or events. This could involve capturing identifying information about the driver (names, drivers license numbers, etc.) on the stop form for subsequent spot checks. As an alternative it may be possible to connect stop records with their corresponding video records.

Data collection systems should be able to determine the completeness of the data set. In most departments there is no single repository wherein all police/citizen contacts are recorded. Often citations, arrests, warnings, case reports and field interviews are filed in separate databases or places. As a result it is difficult to determine whether the stops recorded in the racial profiling data set include all police/citizen contacts, regardless of their nature or outcome. The expense associated with merging multiple existing data sets for the sole purpose of measuring the completeness of racial profiling data is likely not justifiable. Alternatively, it is possible to compare subsets of the racial profiling data with corresponding existing datasets. For example, the number of arrests reported on officers' activity reports should closely approximate the number of arrests reported by officers in the racial profiling dataset.

The quality of a data set is directly related to how much training officers receive on how to use it. Racial profiling data collection is just like any new reporting requirement. For example, when officers were first required to complete reports on domestic violence incidents training was essential. Prior to starting a racial profiling data collection it is essential to provide officers with sufficient training. Questions like what types of contacts should be reported, how the data will be reported and many more should be answered in the training program.

Clearly written policies improve data collection. Clearly written policies governing data collection are closely related to training. Beyond this it is essential for departments to provide officers with written direction on the rules and procedures relating to racial profiling data collection. This necessarily includes a workable definition of racial profiling, the kinds of stops that should be recorded on a stop form and the consequence of noncompliance.

Pilot test the data collection system prior to using it for real. Survey researchers call this pre-testing. This process involves testing the actual instrument or system in which the data are to be collected prior to its full implementation. No matter how carefully a data collection system is designed, nearly every pilot test reveals inefficiencies that, uncorrected, seriously threaten the viability of the data set. Ideally, pilot tests should be conducted in an environment that closely approximates the actual data collection environment.

What Information to Collect and Why

The data collected by most racial profiling studies can be organized into three broad categories – information about the persons stopped, information about the stops and information about the officers that conducted the stops. The following (Illustrations Fourteen through Sixteen) outline the variables necessary to conduct a credible stop study. Of course not all variables are equally important. So, the variables in each table are differentiated as either essential or beneficial to a typical racial profiling study. Essential variables are *essential*, because without them the study would not be a racial profiling study. Beneficial variables are *beneficial* because they enhance the ability of an analyst to provide more insight (i.e., explanation) into how the context of a stop affects officer decision making. In addition, brief explanations of each variable's potential value to a racial profiling study are included.

Illustration Fourteen – *Information about the persons stopped.*		
Variables	**Essential/ Beneficial**	**Explanations**
Race	Essential	Without this variable a racial profiling study would not be possible. It is important for the stop data to have the same racial categories as the benchmark.
Ethnicity	Essential	In most cases, ethnicity is separate from race. It is possible to be both Black and Hispanic. Collecting this information separate from race provides the analyst with the flexibility of evaluating the effect of the driver's race, ethnicity and a combination of the two.
Age	Essential	Age is a strong correlate of crime. Younger people tend to be more likely to commit traffic violations and crime, engage in more physical confrontations with the police and drive more frequently. Often a driver's age is the most influential factor in a police officer's decision making.
Gender	Essential	Gender is a strong correlate of crime. Males tend to be more likely to commit traffic violations and crime, engage in physical confrontations with the police and drive more frequently. Often a driver's gender is the most influential factor in a police officer's decision making.
Number of occupants in the car	Essential	Stops involving cars with single occupants are conducted differently than stops involving multiple occupants. Multiple occupant stops take more time, tend to include searches and involve more officers. Each of these are important issues in the racial profiling controversy.
Height	Beneficial	In some situations the physical stature of the driver influences an officer's decision to conduct a search (e.g., pat down), handcuff or extricate a driver from a car.
Weight	Beneficial	In some situations the physical stature of the driver influences an officer's decision to conduct a search (e.g., pat down), handcuff or extricate a driver from a car.
Build	Beneficial	In some situations the physical stature of the driver influences an officer's decision to conduct a search (e.g., pat down), handcuff or extricate a driver from a car.
Clothing	Beneficial	How a driver is dressed when considered within the context of the stop may influence a police officer's enforcement decision. For example, a driver wearing a heavy coat worn on a warm day may justify the officer's decision to conduct a pat down search. Also, visible gang insignia may explain an officer's motivation to initiate a stop.
Demeanor	Beneficial	While a driver's demeanor may influence a police officer's decision, this variable is merely interesting. Besides, measuring demeanor is exceedingly difficult.

Illustration Fifteen – *Information about the stops.*

Variables	Essential/ Beneficial	Explanations
Stop ID Number	Essential	This variable allows the analyst to differentiate between stop events. This number, which may be assigned serially by a form or record number, enables the analysis to develop a case history of each stop. In so doing, the analyst is in a better position to verify the accuracy of police stop data.
Reason (charge)	Beneficial	May explain both the officer's justification for the stop and the disposition (e.g., arrest, citation, warning) of the stop. This variable is only beneficial because it is normally collected in a nondescript manner. For example, a stop for speeding ten miles over the limit on a rural highway is not as serious as the same violation in an occupied school zone.
Severity of the driver's behavior leading to the stop	Essential	In order to correlate (associate) the punitiveness of the stop's disposition (arrest, citation, written warning, verbal warning, or no action) with the dangerousness of the driver's behavior that caused the officer to initiate the stop it is necessary to measure the severity of the charge. With guidance, most police officers would be able to define the severity of the driver's behavior on a ten-point scale.
Outcome	Essential	The outcome of a stop (i.e., arrest, citation, written warning, verbal warning or no action) with respect to the driver's race/ethnicity is an important issue in the racial profiling controversy.
Type of arrest	Essential	It is important to differentiate between discretionary and non-discretionary arrests. In a racial profiling study police officers should not be held accountable for non-discretionary (e.g., warrants, domestic violence, other mandatory arrest situations, etc.) arrests.
Formal charges filed	Essential	Including this "yes/no" variable allows the analysts to determine the legitimacy of an officer's decision to arrest. If the number of actual case filings is substantially equal to the number of arrests then it is difficult to accuse the officer of arbitrary and capricious arrests.
Search conducted	Beneficial	This 'yes/no' variable helps the analyst identify the subset of stops that actually include searches.
Type of search conducted	Essential	Not all searches are created equal. Some are required by law or policy and others are discretionary. Discretionary (e.g., consent) searches are more important to a racial profiling inquiry. This variable allows the analyst to differentiate between the various types of searches.
Consent search requested	Beneficial	This 'yes/no' variable allows the analyst to evaluate both police officer and suspect performance.
Consent search allowed	Beneficial	This 'yes/no' variable allows the analyst to evaluate both police officer and suspect performance.
Search rationale	Essential	When properly coded this variable provides insight into a police officer's actual motivation for conducting a search. The attributes of this variable may be general (e.g., document indicators, vehicle indicators, verbal indicators, etc.) or a more specific literal field where the officers actually write their rationale for conducting the search.
Contraband seized	Essential	While the legality of a search cannot be established by its results, this 'yes/no' variable provides insight into officer productivity.
Type contraband seized	Beneficial	This variable in conjunction with search rationale may be helpful for in evaluating officer search productivity and offender pattern analysis.

Illustration Fifteen - *Continued*

Physical resistance	Beneficial	This variable provides important insight into the context of each stop. It is, however, important to indicate when the physical resistance happened during the stop. For example, physical resistance can either be the cause of or the reason for an officer's decision to arrest. It is also important to distinguish physical resistance from physical confrontation.
Physical confron-tation	Beneficial	This variable provides important insight into the context of each stop. It is, however, important to indicate when the physical confrontation happened during the stop. For example, physical confrontation can either be the cause of or the reason for an officer's decision to arrest. It is also important to distinguish physical confrontation from physical resistance.
Location of the stop	Essential	This variable provides insight into the context of each stop. The policing response varies from place to place depending on the crime rate, calls for service and other factors. Normally, this variable can be either the beat number or a census block or tract number.
Time of day	Essential	This variable provides insight into the context of each stop and may explain officer behavior in an important way. Stops at night are conducted differently than stops during the day, particularly in high crime areas. The best way to record this is with military time.
Day of week	Essential	This variable provides insight into the context of each stop and may explain officer behavior in an important way. If recorded as a date with the month, day and year then most analysts can convert this to the actual day of the week.
Residency of the suspect	Beneficial	This variable allows the department to differentiate between resident and nonresident stops. It helps if the department is using a population based benchmark or to determine if differences exists between resident and nonresident stops.

Illustration Sixteen – *Information about the officers that conducted the stops.*

Variables	Essential/ Beneficial	Explanations
Officers identi-fication number	Beneficial/ Essential	This variable allows the analyst to evaluate stops by individual officers. This information would be essential if the department wants to use an internal benchmark. Because this is controversial among police labor organizations the department may consider issuing officers a confidential personal identification number separate from their actual identification or badge number.
Officer's race/ ethnicity	Beneficial	If used the racial/ethnic categories (e.g., Black, White, Hispanic, etc.) should be the same as used in the stop and benchmark data. There is no evidence however that an officer's race affects who the officer stops.
Officer's age	Beneficial	This variable is often useful in evaluating overall officer performance in consent searches. Older officers tend to conduct fewer and more productive consent searches. There is no evidence that an officer's age affects who the officer stops.
Officer's experience	Beneficial	This variable is often useful in evaluating overall officer performance in consent searches. More experienced officers tend to conduct few and more productive consent searches. There is no evidence that an officer's experience affects who the officer stops.

Illustration Sixteen -*Continued*		
Officer's gender	Beneficial	This variable is sometimes useful for evaluating stops that involved physical resistance or confrontation. There is no evidence that an officer's gender affects who the officer stops.
Officer's physical build	Beneficial	This variable is sometimes useful for evaluating stops that involve physical resistance or confrontation. There is no evidence that an officer's physical build affects who the officer stops.

How Racial Profiling Data Should Be Analyzed

There are two general types of statistics – descriptive and inferential. Each has their own advantages and disadvantages. The decision on which statistical technique to use depends primarily on the level the data are measured. Generally, the availability and precision of statistical techniques increases with the level of measurement. For example, there are very few statistical techniques available for analyzing data collected at the nominal level, like race, gender or reason for the stop. Even when used effectively, these techniques seldom produce definitive results. On the other hand, if the data are collected at the interval or ratio levels the availability of statistical techniques is nearly unlimited. In fact, an analyst can even use data collected at the interval and ratio levels in statistical techniques that are designed specifically for nominally measured variables.

The following section is by no means a definitive discussion on statistical analysis. The techniques described are limited to those commonly used by racial profiling researchers. This section is designed to provide a broad overview of frequently used statistical techniques, and in doing so, enable the reader to be a more informed consumer of statistical analysis.

Descriptive Statistics

Descriptive statistics merely describe what is. Averages, percentages and standard deviations are descriptive statistics (see Illustration Seventeen). Because most of the data collected in a typical racial profiling study is either nominal or ordinal, most analyses are limited to descriptive statistics.

Illustration Seventeen – *Commonly used descriptive statistics.*

Measures of central tendency (averages)

Measure	How calculated	Advantages	Disadvantages	Level of measurement required	Example
Mode	Select the most frequently occurring attribute for a particular variable.	The only measure of central tendency available for nominally measured variables.	May not be representative of the data set if other attributes are nearly as frequent.	Nominal	The most common violation reported by the officers is speeding.
Median	Arrange the values in numerical order and select the one that occurs in the middle. If there is an even number of values, the median is halfway between the middle two values.	Not sensitive to extreme scores or outliers.	May produce a value that is actually does not exist within the data set.	Ordinal Interval Ratio	The median age of individuals stopped is 18.5 years old.
Mean	Divide the sum of all values by the total number of values.	All values within the data set are used to create this measure.	Sensitive to extreme scores or outliers. An overly large or small value can skew the result.	Interval Ratio	When longer lasting stops involving arrests or searches are removed, the average traffic stop last 11.4 minutes.

Illustration Seventeen – Commonly used descriptive statistics. (Continued)

Measures of variability

Measure	How calculated	Advantages	Disadvantages	Level of measurement required	Example
Range	Subtract the highest value from the lowest value	Illustrates the extremes of the data set.	Sensitive to extreme scores or outliers and may not accurately describe the data if there are extremely low or high scores.	Interval Ratio	Speeds observed on Main Street ranged 25 mps, from a low of 20 mph to a high of 45 mph.
Standard deviation	Subtract each value from the mean, square these values and then sum. Divide the result by the total number of values. The square root of this result is the standard deviation.	Standardizes the variation within the data and is not overly sensitive to extreme values.	Tedious to calculate by hand.	Interval Ratio	The standard deviation of the speeds observed on Main Street is 4 mph.

Note: Both the variance and standard deviation are evaluated directly. This means that the higher the numerical value of either one indicates a greater variation among the values in the data set.

Illustration Seventeen – *Commonly used descriptive statistics.* (Continued)

Percentages

Measure	How calculated	Advantages	Disadvantages	Level of measurement required	Example
Percentage	Divide the number of cases of one attribute by the total number of cases within that variable and multiply by 100.	Effective for illustrating the proportional representation of cases within a single variable.	Limited to a single evaluation	Nominal Ordinal Interval Ratio	Eight hundred (66.6 percent) of the 1,200 total drivers stopped are Hispanic.
Percentile	Arrange the values in rank order lowest to highest. Multiply the total number of values by the preferred percentile (from .01 to .99). The result is the position within the list of values of the preferred percentile score.	Illustrates how cases rank when compared to all cases in the data set.	Does not account for extreme scores	Interval Ratio	Officer Jones' score was 97 was at the 80th percentile, meaning that only 20% of all officers taking the promotional exam scored higher.

Inferential Statistics

The use of higher order inferential techniques for racial profiling data is typically limited by the level at which the data are collected. Most of the important data elements (e.g., race, ethnicity, gender, reason for the stop, search conducted or not, contraband, seized or not, etc.) in racial profiling research are nominally measured. Some data (e.g., the outcome of the stop, age category, etc.) are collected at the ordinal level. Because inferential techniques require data collected at either the interval or ratio levels this severely limits the use of more sophisticated inferential techniques. This is unfortunate because only inferential techniques, most notably regression, can tell the analyst how various factors present during the stops might influence a police officer's decision making. Despite this limitation there are three analytical strategies that produce informative results.

The simplest inferential statistics are correlations, often either a Pearson r or a Spearman rho. These statistics tell us the nature and strength of a relationship between two variables, if any. For example, crime rate and length of the stop are likely positively correlated. This means that as the crime rate increases (in the area where the stops occur) the lengths of the stops occurring in that location also increase. This might suggest the appropriate use of an aggressive policing strategy in high crime areas. Alternatively, the number of patrol units assigned to a beat and the incidence of vehicular burglaries may be negatively correlated. This means that if more officers are assigned to a beat then the number of vehicular burglaries decreases.

Correlation, however, is not cause. Just because two variables are correlated does not mean that one caused the other. For example, African-Americans, when compared to their overall proportion of the driving population, are often over-represented in stops. This appears to suggest that African-American drivers are more likely to be stopped because they are African-American. This conclusion is erroneous because it violates a long-standing procedure for establishing a causal relationship. To establish a causal relationship, or to say that one factor is the cause of another, three rules must be satisfied. First, the cause must precede the effect, or result. If being African-American is alleged to be the cause of being stopped then the driver's race must have "happened" before the stop. Of course, in this case the rule is satisfied because an individual's race is determined well before driving age. Second, the cause and effect must be correlated or related. This means that the cause and effect must happen together in a predictable pattern. In this case to establish correlation the analyst must prove that being African-American actually increases the likelihood of being stopped. In other words, if a police officer simultaneously observes a Caucasian, African-American, Hispanic, Native American and Asian driver committing the same violation then the officer is more likely to stop the African-American driver. More importantly, this also assumes that the officer is able to actually observe the driver's race/ethnicity prior to the stop and then select drivers to stop based on their race/ethnicity. Given the limitations associated with most racial profiling data it is very difficult to satisfy this particular causal rule. Third, all plausible alternative explanations of the results must be eliminated. It may very well be that African-American drivers are over-represented in traffic stops because they are inadvertently subjected to higher levels of police observation. Patrol resources are assigned on the basis of need, usually defined by crime rate. Crime rates tend to be higher in densely populated and lower socioeconomic parts of town. In many communities racial minorities are over-represented in neighborhoods with these characteristics. As a result, African-American drivers may be inadvertently subjected to higher levels of police surveillance and therefore more likely to be observed violating the law.

Chi square, an inferential technique well suited for nominally measured data, is often used to determine whether actual stopping patterns are consistent with predicted stopping patterns. For example, if 10 percent of the overall driving population is African-American then we would expect (all things being equal) that 10 percent of the stops made by police officers would involve African-American drivers. But what if the percentage of stops involving African-American drivers is 15 percent? Is this enough to conclude that African-American drivers are over-represented in stops? Is this enough of a difference to suggest that the police are guilty of racial profiling? Likely not, but a Chi square model comparing the racial/ethnic proportions of the overall driving population (the predicted stopping pattern) with the stopped population (the actual pattern) will produce a statistic that may indicate one or more racial/ethnic group is over-represented enough to suggest a problem.

Interpreting the Chi square statistic is tricky and imprecise. The model does not actually indicate (statistically) which group is over- or under-represented. The model does not provide a benchmark percentage that if exceeded would provide statistical support for a finding that one or more groups are over-represented in stops. The statistic (if statistically significant) only indicates that at least one group is either over- or under-represented.

As a result, the interpretation of the results is subjective.

It is up to the analyst's judgment to determine
1. which group(s) are over- or under-represented, and
2. whether the percentage differences are enough to suggest a pattern of abuse.

The Chi square technique, despite its limitations, has proven to be useful in racial profiling studies that use internal benchmarks. This research attempts to compare the stopping performances of police officers who are similarly assigned. Internal benchmarks, often called early warning systems, are discussed in more detail later in this chapter.

Regression models are effective tools for determining the relative influence of various factors on an outcome. For example, a regression model would tell a researcher how education, years of experience and the number of hours worked per week each affect income. Unfortunately, regression models require a continuous outcome (or dependent) variable. This means that the outcome variable (income in the previous example) must have multiple levels and be measured at the interval or ratio levels. In racial profiling results, outcome variables (e.g., arrest/no arrest, consent search conducted/no consent search conducted, contraband seized/no contraband seized, etc.) are often not continuous. These are called binary or dichotomous variables. Fortunately, there is an analytical option. A logistic regression model allows a researcher to determine the relative influence of various factors on a binary outcome variable. For example, using a logistic regression model an analyst could determine how (or even if) the crime rate in the neighborhood where the stop occurred, the time of day the stop occurred, and the number of occupants in the car influenced an officer's decision to initiate a consent search. With sufficiently detailed data a logistic regression can even produce a profile of searches that are more likely to produce contraband seizures, thereby improving overall officer productivity.

Develop an Early Warning System

Police departments routinely collect immense amounts of information. In most cases this information is vital to the ongoing evaluation of their department's effectiveness and efficiency. Often police officers are required to complete regular reports on their activities as a means to assess their productivity. Few policing leaders would argue that their departments should collect more information, but many would agree that their departments could make better use of the information they collect. More specifically, policing leaders need timely data that is relevant to evaluating the performance of their departments, not just more data.

In response to this need, many departments have developed early warning systems designed to provide real time access to various productivity measures. These programs also are able to identify trends that, left unattended, could result in more serious problems. For example, one department monitors the frequency and nature of citizen complaints filed (formally and informally) against individual officers in an effort to identify officers who may be developing behavioral problems.

In 2003, Sam Walker, then a professor at the University of Nebraska at Omaha, proposed using early warning systems in racial profiling research (Walker 2003). This system relies on the use of an internal benchmark, wherein individual police officer performance is compared with similarly assigned officers. For example, let's assume that over the course of a year, twenty different officers were assigned to work the day shift in a particular beat or neighborhood. Over time these officers stop records would establish a pattern for that shift and beat. Let's further assume that during this year, twelve percent of the stops made by these officers involved Hispanic drivers. A closer analysis of the data might reveal that thirty percent of the stops made by one of the twenty officers assigned to this beat/shift involve Hispanic drivers. Of course this does not definitively prove that this officer is guilty of racial profiling. It may be that this officer, unlike his similarly situated peers, is fluent in Spanish and is often asked to handle cases involving Spanish-speaking motorists. At the very least this analysis provides a policing administrator with evidence of a possible problem.

Creating an early warning system to monitor potential racial profiling behaviors is no easy task. At the writing of this text, only one major racial profiling analysis has been conducted using an internally developed benchmark (Withrow, Dailey & Jackson 2009). Even then the data were insufficient in measuring all of the patrol assignment variations that could identify similarly assigned officers. For example, these researchers could not differentiate between officers generally assigned to patrol duties from officers assigned to special task forces like gang suppression units. It would be unfair to evaluate officers on the basis of beat and shift alone.

Despite their complicated nature, early warning systems that use internally developed benchmarks offer considerable advantages over traditional racial profiling studies that rely on externally developed benchmarks.

First, early warning systems provide ongoing racial profiling surveillance. Most departments collect data over a defined time frame, issue a report, hold a press conference, implement a training program, make a few administrative or policy changes, and then abandon future studies. This is unfortunate because these departments will never be able to determine whether the changes they made or the training they offered changed their overall stopping practices.

Second, the internal benchmark feature of an early warning system eliminates the measurement error associated with externally developed estimates of the racial/ethnic proportions within the driving population. All externally developed benchmarks (discussed in the previous chapter) contain measurement error. The presence of this error calls into question the accuracy of the research results. Internal benchmarks do not estimate the racial/ethnic proportions within the driving population and therefore attempt to establish an acceptable percentage of stops for each race or ethnic group. Instead the benchmark is established by the stops themselves. For example, if fifteen percent of the stops made by a group of similarly assigned officers over the course of a year involve African-American drivers then that is the benchmark that these particular officers must be consistent with in order to avoid administrative scrutiny.

Third, early warning systems provide the department with an opportunity to identify potentially errant officers. Most racial profiling data collections do not associate specific stops with individual officers. Even when they do the results of most racial profiling studies are reported aggregately. While understandable, this practice eliminates the department's ability to identify an individual officer who may be exhibiting racial profiling behaviors. Early warning systems can identify officers who tend to stop inordinately high percentages of drivers within one racial/ethnic category when compared to their similarly assigned peers. Of course these results are not definitive evidence of racial profiling. They are merely indicators that can be used for routine administrative reviews or even during an internal affairs investigation.

Fourth, early warning systems can identify potential training needs. For example, such systems might identify officers who have a high frequency of citizen complaints, a low percentage of contraband seizures pursuant to consent searches, or inappropriate citation to warning ratios. All of these suggest potential training needs and may provide administrators with an opportunity to intervene and address officer performance problems proactively.

Of course early warning systems are not a panacea. They are inordinately difficult to set up and maintain. Given the complex and unpredictable nature of routine police deployment and allocation it is very difficult to identify the factors (e.g., beat, shift, assignment, day of week, etc.) that define similarly assigned or situated officers. Early warning systems are controversial because they require police officers to associate their identification numbers with the stops they make. In some communities the police officers' organizations have successfully barred departments from requiring officers to enter their identification numbers on racial profiling stop forms. Finally, early warning systems will not work if officers collaborate inappropriately to create an artificial internal benchmark. The probability of this is low because such collaboration would involve multiple officers over an extended time frame.

Value of a Research Partner

Only within the past two decades have police departments begun to appreciate the value of trained researchers and analysts. The advent of COMPSTAT, geographic information systems, and new crime analysis techniques has convinced policing leaders of the importance of individuals with strong analytical and statistical skills. Even so, many departments do not have the personnel necessary to adequately conduct a rigorous racial profiling study or to analyze the complicated data these studies produce. Even the departments fortunate enough to have access to such personnel are wary to use internal resources because they may be perceived by outsiders to be biased. As a result the value of a research partner, independent from the department, is well established.

To be effective, a research partner hired to assist the department with a racial profiling study should have three well-developed skills sets.

First, the research partner should be informed of generally accepted research methodologies. This means that the research partner has the ability to develop solid research questions and create data collection strategies that will produce the information in the format necessary to respond to the project's needs.

Second, the research partner should have strong analytical skills. Most racial profiling analyses require the use of several analytical strategies including the various measures of central tendency and variability, the comparison of percentages and even the creation of complicated inferential models.

Finally, the research partner should have a thorough understanding of police patrol procedures. Ideally, the analyst should have some actual experience as a police practitioner. Knowing how to collect and analyze data is not enough. It is critically important for the research partner to know the context from which the data come. For example, an analyst may identify an officer who stops an inordinately high percentage of drivers from one particular racial category. On its face this may seem alarming. However, when the analyst realizes that this officer is assigned to a beat that is principally populated by individuals of that racial category this finding is not so alarming.

3

The Importance of Managing Discretion and Controlling Consent Searches

P olice officers enjoy a tremendous amount of discretionary authority. Upon observing a violation a police officer may either initiate one of several enforcement actions or merely ignore it and move on. Of course there are exceptions. Certain violations, such as domestic violence and driving while intoxicated, require officers to initiate an arrest. Often department policies require officers to conduct certain enforcement actions in specific situations, such as searches pursuant to an arrest or inventory searches of impounded vehicles. But for the most part the decision to initiate an enforcement action, most importantly the decision to initiate a stop, is solely that of the street level officer.

Police officer decision making typically occurs at a distance from active supervision. Supervisors are usually not in a position to scrutinize every decision made by a police officer. While active supervision is necessary in some situations, such as high speed vehicular chases, for the most part the police are left alone, and even encouraged, to use their discretionary authority as they see fit.

A common saying in business is, "nothing happens until somebody sells something." Criminal justice has a similar saying, "nothing happens until a police officer decides to stop somebody." While it is possible for an individual to enter the criminal justice process without initially being stopped by the police, most defendants enter the formal criminal justice process following a traffic stop or some other police/citizen interaction. The police, therefore, are the primary gatekeepers of the criminal justice process.

Police administrators are highly resistant to limits on the discretionary authority of their officers. They don't want to "tie their officers' hands" by imposing administrative limits on discretionary decision making. A police chief will not likely prohibit officers from initiating traffic stops, even for minor or technical violations, especially when the officers have a hunch about a suspect. After all, hunches are sometimes right and some important arrests come from seemingly benign traffic stops.

Police officers have nearly unfettered discretionary authority, make decisions alone without benefit of active supervision, and create the most common entrée into the formal criminal justice process. This is precisely why police patrol operations are so heavily scrutinized by the courts and disparaged by critics of the police.

The use, or more specifically the alleged misuse, of discretionary authority is an important issue within the racial profiling controversy. The accusation is that the police are inconsistent in their enforcement approach, particularly with respect to the race or ethnicity of the individuals they encounter. The police are often accused of vigorously enforcing minor violations of the law when a minority suspect is involved, while ignoring serious violations committed by non-minority suspects. In a rather infamous racial profiling case the officer is alleged to have responded when the violator questioned the legality of the stop, "That string holding up your pine tree air freshener is obstructing your rear view mirror, and that is a serious violation of the law."

Police administrators are justified in allowing their officers the discretionary authority to make most enforcement decisions. When police officers are allowed to exercise discretion they develop a highly refined street sense that is useful in identifying potential criminal violations and indeed essential to their safety. After all, even stops for dirty license plates sometimes produce substantial contraband seizures. Unfortunately, the legitimacy of a police stop is seldom evaluated within its actual context. The car with the dirty license plate may have been observed leaving the scene of burglary or may be occupied by a person fitting the description of a known criminal suspect. These contextual factors are seldom reported in the officer's report because they are ancillary to the objectively legal justification for the stop. In some cases, identifying contextual factors as an important part of the police officer's decision to stop may even threaten the legal justification for the stop. In the absence of these factors, stops for relatively minor violations of the traffic code are often perceived to be illegitimate by the general public. The purpose of this chapter is to provide some guidance into how police administrators might achieve a balance between the necessity of police officer discretionary authority and the perception of legitimacy in police officer decision making.

The Power Dynamics of the Traffic Stop

Police patrol operations are the foundation of most departments' enforcement programs. Crime suppression and detection, drug interdiction, intelligence gathering and other vital law enforcement processes are heavily dependent on patrol officers making a lot of traffic stops.

The value of traffic stops to a department's overall enforcement program is enhanced by three factors.

1. *Comprehensive traffic codes provide potential probable cause generating events.*

There are thousands of things a person can do with, in, or to a vehicle that produce the probable cause necessary for a police officer to initiate a traffic stop. Some traffic violations, like speeding, are common, while others, like an obstructed rearview mirror, are rather rare. Not all violations are equally threatening to public safety. Following too close is more dangerous than a dirty license plate. But all violations provide police officers with a legal means to stop and detain a motorist.

2. *Violating the traffic code is nearly inevitable.*

Very few motorists can honestly say that they never violate the traffic code. Those making such a claim are likely unaware that some of the things they do everyday are in fact violations of the traffic code. Most drivers commit at least several violations every time they get behind the wheel. Experienced police officers know that if followed long enough, and usually not very long at all, most drivers will commit at least one traffic violation. When they do, the police have the legal justification to initiate a traffic stop.

3. *When stopped, most drivers will allow the police to conduct a consent search.*

It is possible that some drivers are not aware that they can deny a police officer's request to conduct a consent search. Most drivers, however, are cognizant of this Constitutional right but will allow such searches anyway. Maybe these drivers think that if they refuse the police will continue the stop and seek a search warrant? Even drivers who are aware that they are in possession of illegal substances will readily give the police permission to search. Maybe these drivers think their willingness will erase the police officer's suspicion? Regardless, most drivers, when asked, will readily submit to being searched.

These three factors combine to form a power dynamic that is important to the racial profiling controversy. **Experience teaches a police officer two important realities.** *First,* most people, when asked, will consent to a search. *Second,* most drivers will readily commit a violation of the traffic code. As a result, when a police officer has a desire to investigate a suspicious circumstance, he need only observe the vehicle or person for a short while before he is provided with an objectively legitimate reason for initiating a traffic stop that will likely include the driver's consent to conduct a search.

Factors Affecting a Traffic Stop's Perceived Legitimacy

The legitimacy of a traffic stop is perceived from at least three perspectives.

First, there is the legal justification for the stop. Did the driver actually commit the alleged violation? If the answer to this question is yes then the stop is at least legally justified. Even if the violator is found not guilty of the charge, the stop may still be legally legitimate if the officer acted in good faith.

Second, although inappropriate, whether the stop and/or subsequent search produced evidence of a more serious law violation often determines the subjective legitimacy of the stop. The objective legitimacy of any criminal justice process is never defined by its result. The legitimacy of a criminal justice decision, including a stop and search, is always defined by the legality of its process. Illegally seized evidence is worthless in a criminal proceeding. And, on the other side of the coin a legal stop and search is not made illegal because it fails to produce evidence of a more serious violation. Even so, the public perception of a stop or search's legitimacy is improved when the police are right and diminished when the police are wrong.

Third, ultimately the legitimacy of a traffic stop or search is determined from the violator's perspective. Numerous factors, many of which are well outside the control of the police officer, affect a violator's perception of a traffic stop. Things like the violator's previous experiences with the police, the violator's mood at the time of the stop, and even the general perception of the police among the violator's friends, family and reference group affect the violator's perception of a stop's legitimacy. The research on how violators perceive traffic stops is rather limited. The most credible study was conducted in England by Quinton, Bland and Miller in 2000. According to these researchers, for a traffic stop to be perceived as legitimate it must have four qualities (see Illustration Eighteen).

Illustration Eighteen – *Factors affecting the perceived legitimacy of a traffic stop.*

1. To ensure public trust and confidence, stops must be perceived to be carried out for good reasons. The stated reason for the stop should be perceived to be important and consistent with a real public safety need. Ideally, the officer should articulate this public safety concern to the violator.

2. Stops and searches must be based on an appropriate legal or policy standard. They must adhere to generally accepted guidelines of police procedure and not appear to be arbitrary or capricious.

3. Stops must be perceived to be an effective strategy in the pursuit of a legitimate law enforcement need. This means that stops are targeted to maximize contact with active offenders and minimize contact with law abiding citizens.

4. The violator's perception of an officer's attitudes and behaviors can affect the perceived legitimacy of the stop. Discourtesy, foul language and incomplete explanations appear to reduce the violator's perception of the stop's legitimacy.

Managing Discretion

One solution to the racial profiling controversy may lie in the control of police discretion through policy. In the absence of clearly stated enforcement policies police officers tend to develop personal enforcement habits. Nearly every police officer has a "pet" violation that warrants his attention and action. The justifications for these decisions are seldom well documented and few officers are held accountable for them. This does not, however, suggest that these enforcement criteria are illegitimate. Holding officers accountable for their decisions, especially highly discretionary stops involving non-moving and equipment violations, may be the answer.

That, however, is easier said than done. It is not likely possible to develop an enforcement policy that will be relevant in every situation a police officer might encounter. Furthermore, it would not be advisable to limit an officer's discretionary authority with absolute rules on when and why drivers can be stopped and for what violations. Police officers are after all commissioned to enforce the entire breadth of the law within their jurisdiction. The solution to managing discretion may lie in three parts, each of which contributes to mitigating racial profiling problems.

Write Clear Racial Profiling Policies and Procedures

Write clear policies that prohibit enforcement decisions based principally on the race or ethnicity of a driver. Of course, writing a policy is one thing. Implementation is another. *The research suggests that policies prohibiting racial profiling are more effective when they are 1) developed collaboratively, 2) well defined, and 3) visibly enforced.*

Model policies are readily available from various state, regional, national and even international law enforcement associations and organizations. Reviewing these model policies is a good first step, but wholesale adoption of model policies almost never results in a successful implementation. There is simply too much variation in police operations between jurisdictions. Policy should be developed to meet the needs of the entire community. This requires the involvement of various community stakeholders, policy makers, command officers, and most especially patrol officers. While complicated, time-consuming and even at times frustrating, such collaboration nearly always results in a more workable policy.

It is important to define the key terms of any policy. While the terms "racial profiling" and "race-based policing" are likely familiar to most officers, the exact meaning of these terms must be clearly defined within the policy. For example, the research suggests that police officers are very good at recognizing racial profiling behaviors when presented with enforcement scenarios involving racial or ethnic minority drivers. When these scenarios are changed to involve non-minority drivers, police officers are not as likely to recognize racial profiling behaviors (Withrow 2004). In other words, for many police officers racial profiling means driving while black or driving while brown, but not driving while white. It is therefore important for the policy to communicate that racial profiling occurs when any race/ethnicity is used as the primary criteria for initiating a stop.

Finally, there is very little evidence that the racial profiling controversy has changed the way police officers work or police departments are managed (Shultz and Withrow 2004). Following the publication of a racial profiling study, most departments promulgate a policy prohibiting racial profiling, require officers to attend racial sensitivity/diversity training, and then move on to the next issue. Complaints against police officers for violations of a department's racial profiling controversy are seldom sustained. The inability to sustain racial profiling complaints may be due to the difficulty associated with actually proving that a police officer initiated a stop because of the driver's race or ethnicity. Or, more likely, police officers are seldom guilty of such transgressions. Eventually, however, a policy's perceived inability to identify and sanction errant officers, will erode public confidence to the point where additional inquiries are demanded by political leaders and community stakeholders, thereby resurrecting the controversy all over again. This does not suggest the need for sacrificial lambs. Police officers should never be subjected to frivolous administrative inquires just to satisfy the demands of their critics. The operative issue here is responsiveness. Citizen complaints, and particularly those involving allegations of racial profiling, should be investigated promptly and thoroughly. The results of these investigations should be disseminated and openly shared with the larger community, within the boundaries of protocol or statute. Ideally, the complaint process for racial profiling cases should be proactive

rather than reactive. For example, some progressive departments require officers to initiate the complaint process
against themselves (i.e., report an accusation of racial profiling) even when a citizen merely suggests that a stop was
motivated by race or ethnicity.

Develop Workable Enforcement Criteria and Tolerances

Because police stops are critically important to a department's overall enforcement program, it is important to provide
officers with guidance on the kinds of violations and driver
behaviors that should warrant their attention. These violations and behaviors should be consistent with the department's overall enforcement objectives. For example, if fatality
accidents caused by speeding increase then the department
should encourage officers to vigorously enforce speeding
violations. Other enforcement criteria may be developed to
respond to the public safety specific needs of a jurisdiction.
These classic problem-oriented policing approaches are
appropriate responses to bona fide public safety problems.

The connection between speed enforcement and traffic
fatalities is rather easy to defend. Of more concern to the
racial profiling controversy are the individual stops that are
seemingly irrelevant to overall public safety. Stops for relatively minor violations are almost always considered frivolous
from the violator's perspective. Getting stopped for a dirty
license plate usually results in a comment like, "Why are you
bothering me instead of looking for the real criminals?" from
an incensed violator.

Beyond the need to logically connect stops with enforcement strategies there is a practical need to limit officer
discretion. Police departments seldom have enough officers to
maintain desired response times, especially during high call
for service times of the week. Controlling officer discretion,
and particularly restricting stops for minor violations, main-
tains officer availability during peak demand periods.

Some enforcement criteria are objectively simple to
develop. Speed tolerances can be expressed numerically, like
"No officer shall issue a citation to a motorist operating a
motor vehicle less than five miles per hour over the posted
speed limit." This policy can even be customized to exclude
certain flagrant violations like speeding in a school zone or a
residential area. The department may even desire to add the
phrase "unless the motorist's behavior is particularly flagrant"
to allow officers to stop particularly dangerous drivers

operating within the enforcement tolerance. The objective of this policy is to prohibit officers from spending time with low risk drivers so they will be available to respond to more flagrant threats to public safety.

Enforcement criteria designed to reduce the perception of racial profiling have a similar objective. These policies should be designed to maximize contact with serious law violators and, thereby, minimize contact with low risk violators and non-violators. In addition, these policies should reduce the frequency of pretextual stops and other stops designed principally to provide the police with an opportunity to conduct a consent search. Quite possibly the easiest way to do this would be to prohibit stops for non-flagrant violations. Such a policy may even prohibit officers from making stops for which the violator would not likely receive a citation. The importance of issuing a citation or written warning as a means to mitigate racial profiling complaints is discussed in a later chapter.

In order to avoid the possibility that police officers, in deference to the enforcement policy, may avoid making stops for minor violations that may produce evidence of a more serious violation, it may be advisable to add an exception. The enforcement policy could contain a provision whereby a police officer would be allowed to initiate a stop for a non-flagrant violation when "other" factors are present that produce reasonable suspicion. Such a provision, for example, would allow an officer to initiate a traffic stop for a minor violation when a suspicious vehicle is observed in a high crime area.

Conduct Regular Audits

Regularly reviewing individual officer stopping patterns provides important insight into a department's actual enforcement behavior. Following the release of a racial profiling study's results, most departments move on to other issues. This is likely a mistake. The racial profiling controversy has a very bad habit of resurrecting itself, especially following the public disclosure of an event involving the police and the minority community. Regular and routine surveillance of information that is relevant to the racial profiling controversy will provide administrators with a means to evaluate their officer's performance with the organization's overall enforcement goals.

Many departments have maintained systems for reviewing police stop information for decades. These systems typically evaluate the number of stops made by each officer, by shift, day, time, violation, and even miles driven between stops. Some systems even measure officer productivity in various stop events, like consent searches and contraband seizures. A few systems attempt to identify individuals who are stopped multiple times. Most systems, however, do not provide the insight necessary to identify potential racial profiling behaviors because many of these behaviors are counterintuitive. For example, alleged racial profiling victims frequently complain because the officer did not issue them a citation. Normally, a violator would consider this a good thing. Unfortunately, to some violators, the officer's decision to not issue a citation is considered evidence of the stop's illegitimate nature. "If my driving was bad enough for the officer to stop me, then why did I not get a ticket?" is a frequent question expressed by alleged racial profiling victims. This perspective is particularly common among minority drivers who are stopped frequently and never issued a citation. See Illustration Nineteen for a list of evaluative criteria designed to identify possible racial profiling behaviors in the stops made by individual police officers.

Illustration Nineteen – *Indicators of possible racial profiling behaviors.*

1. A high percentage of stops for relatively minor traffic or equipment violations.
2. A high proportion of stops (when compared to similarly assigned officers) involving minority drivers.
3. A high percentage of stops that include consent searches or requests to conduct consent searches.
4. A high proportion of searches (when compared to similarly assigned officers) involving minority drivers.
5. A low proportion of searches (particularly consent searches) that result in the seizure of contraband or evidence of another violation.
6. A high percentage of stops resulting in warnings or no action.
7. A high percentage of arrests subsequent to a traffic stop that do not include information on why the violator was stopped.
8. A high percentage of arrests that do not result in an actual filing of charges.
9. A low number of stops (when compared to similarly assigned officers) when assigned to neighborhoods or beats that are populated predominantly by racial or ethnic minorities.
10. Frequent citizen complaints alleging racial bias.

Controlling Consent Searches

For two reasons, consent searches are the most notorious part of the racial profiling controversy. Because they are not tied to an independent finding of proof (i.e., probable cause by a magistrate) consent searches are highly discretionary. A police officer may request consent to conduct a search for any reason, or for no reason at all. In fact, having no reason at all is usually a more defensible position than when an officer offers a justification for the search that does not meet the level of probable cause. Because they are arbitrary, consent searches are considered by some to be little more than a legal means to harass citizens. Second, consent searches seldom produce contraband. A very small percentage of consent searches actually result in a seizure of contraband or in finding evidence of more serious criminal activity.

While the legality of a search is never determined by its result, when a search fails to produce contraband or evidence of criminal activity it is perceived to be unreasonable.

Consent searches are an important part of a comprehensive enforcement program. When handled properly consent searches are a highly efficient method to remove hazardous contraband from a community, locate evidence of more serious criminal activity, and collect relevant intelligence. Consent searches provide the police with a low-cost means to expand the effectiveness of routine traffic stops. On the other hand, from a social cost perspective, consent searches are very expensive. When large numbers of drivers, particularly minority drivers, are frequently and unproductively searched a police department's public image is tarnished (Harris 2002). As a result, it is prudent to control consent searches using three strategies.

Formalize the Consent Search Process

Formalizing the consent process will protect civil liberties as well as result in a more judicious use of the consent search. In 1966, the United States Supreme Court imposed a requirement on police officers during custodial interrogations. In *Miranda v. Arizona* the Court ruled that evidence obtained during a custodial interrogation would be inadmissible in a criminal proceeding unless the police first informed the suspect of his Constitutional rights. The ubiquitous *Miranda* warnings are now a routine part of police procedures. But, in 1966, most policing practitioners worried that informing suspects of their rights prior to a custodial interrogation would make criminal confessions extinct. After all, who in their right mind would confess when they know everything they say might be held against them in a court of law? For a while they were right, cases closed by a confession did decrease during the next few years. But, by the end of the decade the percentage of cases closed by a confession was essentially equal to pre-*Miranda* levels.

Miranda is unquestionably the most important legal ruling in the history of American policing. It was a wake-up call of sorts in that it called attention to the harshness of police interrogation techniques and abusive behaviors within the American policing profession. *Miranda* and other important criminal procedure cases arising out of the activist Warren Court convinced political leaders, notably President Lyndon B. Johnson, to create the Law Enforcement Assistance Administration. Research and operational grant funds from the LEAA caused a metamorphosis in American policing and vastly improved the professional nature of police work. In a similar way the current research and operational grant funding emphasis on community/problem oriented policing at the federal level is affecting, although to a lesser degree, how police organizations distribute resources. The Law Enforcement Education Program, part of the LEAA, also encouraged thousands of police officers to pursue higher education. In the long-run *Miranda* is directly responsible for improving the policing profession.

Consumption is partly based on cost. We purchase more ground beef than steak because ground beef cost less, offers more preparation options and provides essentially the same nutritional benefit. Cost is not necessarily the same thing as price. Cost can also be defined as inconvenience. A pair of trousers sold by an Internet-based clothing company may cost less than in a department store, but, will they fit right? If not, can I replace them or return them for a refund, and at what cost? If you really need a pair of trousers, it is likely easier to just go to the mall. One thing about cost is for certain. The more things cost the less we will buy them. A corollary to this rule is, inconvenience reduces consumption.

Our experience with *Miranda* and knowledge of how cost affects consumption are potentially useful in the racial profiling controversy. Formalizing the consent search process by voluntarily imposing *Miranda*-like procedures will make the consent search more inconvenient. In doing so, individual police officers will be less likely to initiate a consent search without at least some assurance of its potential to identify contraband or produce evidence of criminal behavior. In other words, making the consent search inconvenient will reduce officers who use it as a "fishing expedition." Such a policy would require police officers to inform citizens of their rights under the law, most notably their right to refuse, prior to requesting a citizen's consent for a search. The policy should also require officers to secure the citizen's signature on a form similar to that used by investigators prior to a custodial interrogation (see Illustration Twenty).

This policy will strengthen the legality of the process and enhance the admissibility of evidence discovered during a consent search. The typical consent search request is, "Do you mind if I search your car?" If the citizen's response is "no," has the officer been granted consent? Did the citizen intend to say "No, I don't mind," therefore giving consent, or "No, you may not search my car"? If the citizen's response is "yes," has the officer been granted consent? Did the citizen intend to say "Yes, I mind," therefore denying consent, or "Yes, you may search my car"? This is precisely why the *Miranda* warnings are written on a standard form and signed by a citizen prior to a custodial interrogation. An individual's signature on a form underneath the *Miranda* warnings removes any reasonable doubt on whether the consent to search was granted voluntarily by an informed citizen.

There might be some concern that formalizing the consent search process, particularly informing citizens of their right to refuse, will reduce the number of consent searches. As previously mentioned, a similar concern was expressed in 1966 regarding the effect of the *Miranda* warnings on confessions. In the years immediately following the *Miranda* ruling, the percentage of cases closed by a confession did decrease. After the *Miranda* warnings became a routine part of police procedures, the percentage of cases closed by a confession returned to pre-*Miranda* levels. Formalizing the consent search process by voluntarily imposing *Miranda*-like procedures will likely follow the same pattern. The percentage of citizens granting consent to be search may decrease until the formal process becomes more routine.

Illustration Twenty – *Consent search Miranda warnings.*

➢ In a moment I am going to ask for your permission to search your car.

➢ Anything I find during this search can be used against you in a court of law.

➢ You have the right to refuse my request to search your car, and your refusal cannot be used against you.

➢ Your refusal to consent to a search cannot be used as proof that you have something to hide if I chose to ask a judge for a search warrant.

➢ You also have the right to limit the areas of your car I am allowed to search.

➢ You may revoke your consent at any time, even after I have started.

➢ May I now have permission to search your car?

Separate Stops and Searches

Separating the consent search request from the justification for the stop improves the search's perceived legitimacy. In deciding *Whren v. United States* a unanimous United States Supreme Court ruled that evidence from a consent search is admissible even when the justification for the stop is pretextual as long as the pretext is a legitimate violation. In this case, the detectives wanted to search the defendant's vehicle after they observed it leaving a known crack house. Absent probable cause of illegal drug possession, the detectives admitted that they followed the defendants long enough in the hope of observing a traffic violation, initiating a stop and then requesting a consent search. It worked.

The *Whren* decision is commonly, but mistakenly, credited with creating the pretextual stop, and therefore contributing to the racial profiling controversy. Fact is, pretextual stops have been an important policing strategy for generations. Pretextual stops were not created by the *Whren* decision, only validated. The *Whren* decision is also consistent with more than two decades of judicial rulings that, as a whole, have expanded police authority to conduct consent searches. A removal of the pretextual stop/consent search tool from the policing tool box is not likely. The concern does not lie in the legality of the pretextual stop/consent search tool, but in the public perception of it as the primary mechanism of racial profiling.

Consider the following two scenarios –

Scenario #1 – Upon initially approaching the violator's vehicle, the officer asked, "Good morning, sir, my name is Officer Joe Smith. Do you mind if I search your car?"

Scenario #2 – After giving the violator a copy of the citation, the officer asked, "Before I leave, would you mind if I searched your car?"

The officers in both scenarios ask essentially the same question. The key difference between them is the timing of the consent search request. The violator in the first scenario is more likely to develop a perception that the actual reason for the stop is the officer's desire to conduct a search. Scenario #1 is typical in media stories wherein citizens allege they are victims of racial profiling. In the vast majority of these cases the citizens report that they are not informed of the reason (i.e., actual traffic violation) they were stopped, much less actually issued a citation, by the officer. In the absence of an explanation and/or a bona fide traffic citation it is easy to understand how some violators might question the validity of the stop described in Scenario #1. On the other hand, in Scenario #2 the officer appears to have a legitimate reason to initiate the stop because a bona fide traffic citation was issued. It would be more difficult for the violator to allege that the stop is illegitimate precisely because a citation was issued. Furthermore, by delaying the consent search request the officer is afforded extra time to more reasonably evaluate indicators of a more serious criminal violation or the potential presence of contraband. Finally, delaying the consent search request to the end of the stop may provide the violator with a false sense of security (i.e., think he got away with something) and thereby *encourage* him to inadvertently provide additional evidence that would further justify the search.

Conduct Regular Audits

Regularly reviewing consent search performance provides important insight into officer productivity and evidence of training needs. In nearly every police department there is at least one officer who seems to have magical powers when identifying vehicles and drivers who are likely to possess contraband. In fact, these officers were the focus of attention when drug courier profiles were initially developed in the 1980s. Alternatively, in nearly every police department there is at least one officer who doesn't have a clue. These officers almost never find contraband or evidence of a criminal violation pursuant to a consent search. Typically, these officers conduct a lot of searches but seize very little contraband. These officers need and deserve the attention of their department's administrators.

The first step is to identify unproductive officers. This is easily accomplished by calculating the percentage of consent searches that actually produce contraband or evidence of a criminal violation (i.e., hit rates) for each officer and then comparing these to the success rate for the overall department. Officers reporting substantially lower hit rates warrant the attention of the department and can be scheduled for evaluation and/or training.

The next step is more complicated. Merely knowing an individual officer's hit rate provides almost no insight into the factors affecting his productivity. Some officers are more perceptive than others and are therefore more likely to recognize the indicators of a successful consent search. Productive officers, however, are not born clairvoyant. They develop their ability to evaluate the probability of a successful consent search through trial and error. They learn from their successes and failures and over time develop considerable skill. For a few officers this skill building exercise is relatively easy, and may even seem instinctual. Most officers need a little help with evaluating their overall long-term performance, especially for infrequent events like consent searches. This can only be achieved by collecting and evaluating detailed information on the factors that influenced the officer's decision to request a consent search. It is important to note that these factors should not be considered the legal justification for the search. Consent searches require no legal justification. This information is collected for the sole purpose of identifying the factors that tend to either increase or decrease the probability of a successful consent search. For example, are younger drivers more or less likely to be in possession of contraband than older drivers? Are searches conducted at night more or less likely to produce evidence of a criminal violation than searches conducted during the day? Are recently replaced fenders more likely to contain drugs?

A comprehensive stop data collection program, such as that described in Chapter 2, will provide the data necessary to evaluate consent search performance. Expanding the attributes for the search rationale variable (see Illustration Fifteen, p. 52) would be particularly useful.

4

The Trap of Deployment and the Risk of Disengagement

A mong teenage boys there is a common belief that red sports cars are more likely to be stopped than duller colored sedans. "If a cop sees two cars, one a red Corvette and the other a blue minivan, each traveling the same speed (over the limit), the cop will always stop the red Corvette" is nearly a proverb among high school drivers. But is it true?

One morning I decided to find out if any evidence existed that supported this proposition. After an exhaustive search of the literature, I found no empirical evidence at all that the color or style of a car affected an officer's stop decision. Feeling somewhat like a myth buster, I left the university for a lunch appointment with my insurance agent. I had recently purchased a new pickup truck and need to change my existing coverage. During our meeting my agent asked me, "What color is your new truck, Doc?" "Red!" I responded. My agent looked over his glasses and with a grim look in his face asked, "Are you sure?" "Yes, why?" I asked. "The rates are higher for red vehicles than for other colors because, for some reason, people who drive red cars are more likely to file a claim" he explained. Turns out, my agent is right. While red cars are not inherently more dangerous, it is true that younger drivers, who are more likely to take risks, tend to choose more vividly colored cars. So, it is not the color, it is something about the person who chooses a red car that increases the probability of a claim. So, as far as my insurance carrier is concerned, my new truck is *maroon*!

There is nothing magic about predicting the probability of getting stopped by a police officer for a traffic violation. Who gets stopped is mostly a function of who gets observed violating the law by a police officer. Other factors may influence the probability of a stop. Issues like the seriousness of the violation, the busyness of the officer, traffic volume, and yes, even the type of car may either increase or decrease the probability of getting stopped. Drivers violate traffic laws all the time, but unless they are actually observed by a police officer, they cannot be stopped. It is reasonable therefore to propose that drivers are more likely to be stopped when they are subjected to a higher level of police observation. This has important consequences to the racial profiling controversy.

Beginning in the 1970s, quite a few criminologists attempted to identify the factors that increase the likelihood that a police officer will make an arrest. These researchers identified various factors that appear to influence the arrest decision. Unfortunately this research was limited to known police/citizen contacts wherein the police were called to intervene. As a result, very little is known about how police officers decide to initiate a contact in the first place. Even less is known about how or why a police officer decides *not* to initiate a contact.

Collectively, the enforcement decisions made by individual police officers have a profound effect on public safety. What the police do and how they do it matters. When confronted with a serious threat to public safety, appropriately deployed police officers are in the best position to improve public safety. For example, a saturation patrol strategy is often effective for suppressing gang activity. Vigorous and concentrated speed enforcement reduces traffic accidents and eventually fatalities. And, a directed patrol program is an appropriate strategy for confronting a localized increase in vehicular burglaries.

If the police can improve public safety when they are appropriately deployed, then, is it also true that public safety can be diminished when the police are inappropriately deployed? Worse yet, what would happen if a substantial number of police officers simply chose not to confront violators? Patrol works because it creates a sense of omnipresence that, to some extent, deters potential violators. Although it happens occasionally, few individuals would knowingly commit a violation when the police are visibly, or even potentially, present. If however, the police consistently ignore violations then the deterrent effect of patrol presence is nonexistent. As a result, violators feel free to openly commit violations and may even be emboldened to do so.

It is of course highly unlikely that the police, in substantial numbers, would merely choose not to enforce the law. The police are much too professional for that. But, how do we explain consistent and significant reductions in police stops during racial profiling studies? Why do police labor associations object when stop data include the officers' identification numbers? If a police officer is afraid of being publically accused of racism merely because the person he stops happens to be a racial or ethnic minority, is it logical that he would avoid contact with minority drivers? We do not know the answers to these questions. There is, however, enough evidence to suggest that the racial profiling controversy may be adversely affecting patrol operations at the individual officer level. The challenge for administrators is to identify and prevent systematic disengagement.

The Deployment Trap

The deployment of patrol resources is among the most important decisions made by police administrators. Crime is not equally distributed throughout a community. Some neighborhoods have more crime and therefore deserve more attention from the police department. Ideally patrol resources should be apportioned to optimize response time and increase the deterrence effect created by police officer visibility. In other words, the police are deployed where they are needed the most.

In many ways, a police administrator's decision on where to deploy policing resources is similar to the decision retailers make while determining where to site a store. Retailers place stores near where the people live who are likely to shop at their stores. Gas stations and convenience stores are on corners. Bait and marine stores are near lakes. Pricey department stores are in upscale neighborhoods. The police, in their mobile 'stores' called patrol cars, go where the crime is most likely to happen.

Deployment Determines Who Gets Stopped

When a police administrator decides when and where to concentrate policing resources, particularly patrol resources, he also inadvertently decides who is most likely to be stopped. Here's why. Drivers do most of their driving within the patrol beat where they happen to live. A short trip to the grocery store or a cross-country drive both start and end in the patrol beat where the traveler lives. Also, drivers who are familiar with their neighborhoods may be more likely to ease through sparsely used stop intersections or drive faster on well-known roads. In doing so, these drivers put themselves at higher risk of being observed violating the traffic law by a police officer. As a result, drivers are more likely to be stopped within or very near the patrol beat in which they reside.

All things being equal (i.e., geographic size, population density, etc.) the residents of a high crime patrol beat (that is assigned more policing resources) have a higher probability of being observed by a police officer. The residents of Beat 3 (see Table 6) have a higher probability of being stopped by a police officer. More patrol officers are assigned to this beat because the calls for service are higher than in the other beats. Even if the Beat 3 residents are equally likely to violate the traffic law as the residents of lower crime beats they are more likely to be stopped because they are subjected to more police officer observation.

Table 6 – *Probability of being stopped based on patrol officer deployment.*

Beat	Area (sq. miles)	Population	Crime rate (calls per service/1,000 residents/ month)	Average number of patrol officers assigned per shift	Number of police officers per residents
1	5.5	5,145	15	2	1:2573
2	5.2	4,489	25	3	1:1496
3	5.1	5,250	100	12	1:438

Because this department's patrol resources are deployed on the basis of legitimate demand nobody would consider this an inappropriate use of resources. After all, the police are supposed to work more in the neighborhoods that are most in need of patrol resources. But, what if we also considered the racial composition[1] of each beat? Here again, we make some initial assumptions. Additional patrol resources are assigned to a beat to equalize the calls for service load per individual officer. If one beat has twice the calls for service load as another then it should be assigned roughly twice as many patrol officers. This means that individual officers, regardless of their beat assignment, have essentially the same call for service demand load and, more importantly, equal opportunity and time to observe and act upon traffic violations. Also, we assume that police officers, regardless of their beat assignment, are equally motivated to initiate traffic stops for the same enforcement objective (e.g., traffic safety). Finally, we assume that all police officers are applying the same enforcement criteria. A flagrant stop sign violation would result in a traffic stop regardless of the beat in which it was observed. Now we revisit our previous demonstration and include the racial composition of each beat (see Table 7).

Table 7 – *Probability of being stopped based on police officer deployment and race of driver.*

Beat	Percent of population that is White	Percent of population that is Black	Crime rate (calls per service/1,000 residents/ month)	Average number of patrol officers assigned per shift	Number of police officers per residents
1	80%	20%	15	2	1:2573
2	50%	50%	25	3	1:1496
3	20%	80%	100	12	1:438

Again, because they experience a higher level of police calls for service, the residents of Beat 3 are subjected to higher levels of police observation and, in turn, a higher probability of being stopped by a police officer. Beat 3 also happens to be principally populated by Black residents. So,

---

[1] To facilitate the demonstration only two racial categories (White and Black) are used.

the part of town with the highest proportion of Black residents also happens to be the part of town that has the highest proportion of policing resources. The residents of Beat 3, who only happen to be Black, are therefore more at risk of being stopped by the police than the residents of other parts of town, namely the beats that are principally populated by White residents.

From this fictitious story important lessons emerge. Racial profiling data is best evaluated at the beat level. Racial profiling data is usually reported at the department wide level. Nearly always these analyses reveal a pattern suggesting minority residents are over-represented in stops occurring throughout the city. Cities, however, are not homogenous with respect to the race or ethnicity of their residents, crime rates and police workload demands. In communities that contain highly segregated beats (with respect to race or ethnicity) that also happen to be highly crime prone it is possible that the stops reported from these beats could skew the city wide results. Sometimes with highly segregated and crime prone beats are removed from the citywide analysis, police stop rates (proportioned by the race or ethnicity of drivers) closely approximate the estimate (i.e., benchmark) of the driving population.

Avoiding a Self-Fulfilling Prophecy

At the heart of the racial profiling controversy is a common misconception that the police look for reasons to stop racial and ethnic minorities because they are more likely to be drug couriers or to possess contraband and evidence of a more serious crime. If this were true then stopping racial and ethnic minorities in higher proportions would make sense. The police, like all professionals, seek ways to improve their efficiency and effectiveness. If the police had a sure-fire way to predict which drivers are more likely to possess evidence of a serious crime then of course they would use it. This would especially be true if the indicator was clearly visible to a police officer. Unfortunately, race and ethnicity are not reliable indicators of drug possession or serious criminal involvement.

Spectators of the racial profiling controversy point to arrest, conviction and incarceration rates as evidence that racial and ethnic minorities are more likely to be involved in serious criminal activity. While it is generally true that racial and ethnic minorities are over-represented in arrests, convictions and incarcerations, there is scant evidence that they are necessarily more likely to be involved in criminal behavior. For example, the findings from two important indicators of criminal behavior are in stark contrast. The National Household Survey of Substance and Drug Abuse finds that the same proportion of Blacks and Whites (12 to 13 percent, respectively) say they use illegal substances. This same survey finds that among users of crack cocaine, 71.3 percent are White, 17.3 percent are Black and 7.9 percent are Hispanic. The United States Sentencing Commission (2000) reports that arrestees for crack cocaine are 5.7 percent White, 84.3 percent Black and 9.0 percent Hispanic. The National Household Survey of Substance Abuse finds that among users of power cocaine, 81.3 percent are White, 7.7 percent are Black and 8.5 percent are Hispanic. The United States Sentencing Commission reports that arrestees for powder cocaine are 18.2 percent White, 30.2 percent Black and 50.5 percent Hispanic. These differences may be in where these particular drugs are bought, sold and consumed. Blacks tend to sell and use crack cocaine and heroin on the street, where police surveillance is more likely intense (STATS 1999) (see Table 8).

Table 8 – *Percentage of (self-reported) users and arrestees by race for crack and powder cocaine.*

	National Household Survey		U.S. Sentencing Commission	
	Powder cocaine users	Crack cocaine users	Powder cocaine arrestees	Crack cocaine arrestees
White	81.3%	71.3%	18.2%	5.7%
Black	7.7%	17.3%	30.2%	84.3%
Hispanic	8.5%	7.9%	50.5%	9.0%

Note: Percentages will not necessarily total 100% because not all racial/ethnic categories are represented.

The perception that minorities are more likely to be drug couriers is also not supported by the empirical evidence. The reason more Blacks are arrested is that more are being searched (Ramirez, McDevitt, and Farrell 2000). There is no credible or objective data that legitimize police attention on one racial group (Covington 2001). Arrest and convictions rates are not measures of criminality, they are measures of police activity (Harris 2002; STATS 1999). In addition, it is true that "Blacks are over-represented among offenders in each category of aggressive crime ..." and that "Blacks are at highly increased risk" for victimization, but 73 percent of criminal episodes are committed by Whites and 27 percent are committed by Blacks (Pallone and Hennessy, 1999, 1).

An analysis of hit rates (i.e., the percent of searches that result in the seizure of contraband or evidence of more serious criminality) from searches also reveals a contrast. Generally, hit rates are not consistently higher for minority drivers than non-minority drivers. In some cases hit rates are higher for non-minorities. Researchers consistently find that Black drivers are less likely to possess contraband than White drivers. These researchers report that the reason minority drivers are arrested more for the possession of contraband (i.e., predominantly drugs) more frequently is because they are searched more often than non-minority drivers (Harris 2002; Knowles, Persico, and Todd 1999; Wise 2003).

The lesson for police administrators who decide where police officers should work is straightforward. The decision on where to deploy officers should be based on indicators of criminal activity or public safety threats that are *created* independent of the police department. Citizen calls for service and citizen reported crime are indicators of crime that occur independent of police activity. When officers are deployed on the basis of these statistics they are responding directly to bona fide community demands for service or indicators of need. Alternatively, arrest, search, stop, citation, or hit rate measures are *created* by police activities. If police are deployed on the basis of the number of arrests or stops they make within a particular beat then the future assignment of officers on the basis of these statistics is a self-fulfilling prophecy. If the police are assigned there, they will work there. If more police are assigned there, then more work will be reported. It may seem that crime is on the upswing when in reality the rise in crime is merely an increase in police activity.

Driving While Not Black

A 2004 re-analysis of the 2001 Wichita Stop Study data demonstrates the importance of analyzing stops at the beat level (Withrow 2004). This analysis compared stops between highly segregated and mixed race beats and revealed several important findings.

First, the number of stops within each beat tended to increase within densely populated beats that experienced high crime (as measured by calls for service). More interestingly, stops did not appear to increase merely because the proportion of Black residents increased. In other words, there was no evidence that the police department was purposely deploying officers to beats that are populated principally by Black residents. Police officers appear to be deployed on the basis of real demand, i.e., denser population and higher crime.

Second, within the beats that are populated predominantly by White residents ("White beats"), Black drivers are consistently over-represented or stopped at higher rates than what the estimate of the driving population predicted. The average percentage of Black residents within the "White beats" is 7.38 percent. The average percentage of Black drivers stopped within the "White beats" is 14.70 percent. Conversely, within the beats that are populated predominantly by Black residents ("Black beats"), White drivers are consistently over-represented in stops. The average percentage of White residents within the "Black beats" is 23.34 percent. The average percentage of White drivers stopped within the "White beats" is 33.33 percent (see Table 9).

Table 9 – *Beat level analysis revealing stop disparity within racially segregated patrol beats.*

Type of Beat	Average percentage of White residents	Average percentage of Black residents	Avg. percentage of stops involving White drivers	Avg. percentage of stops involving Black drivers
Predominantly White	92.72%	**7.38%**	85.02%	**14.70%**
Predominantly Black	**23.34%**	76.66%	**33.33%**	66.68%

Percentages may not sum to 100% due to rounding error.

It appears that race, within the context of the beat, might affect the racial proportion of the individuals who are stopped within the beat. More succinctly, the race an individual *is not* is at least as important as the race an individual is, within the predominant racial context of the beat. From this one could conclude that a White motorist driving in a beat populated primarily by Black residents is just as at risk of being stopped as a Black motorist driving in a beat populated primarily by White residents. These findings produced the following theory.

Theory of Contextual Attentiveness

1. Police officers use the circumstances associated with a distinct episode or location to define what is usual, customary or expected within that particular context.

2. Police officers are differentially attentive toward individuals or behaviors that appear inconsistent with predetermined conceptualizations of what is usual, customary or expected within a particular context.

3. Once an individual or behavior is defined by the police officer as inconsistent with what has been previously determined to be usual, customary or expected within a particular context the police officer may seek a pretext to justify an official encounter.

This theory may explain why a police officer would be suspicious of a juvenile pedestrian in a residential neighborhood during school hours on a school day, but not at all concerned when he sees the same kid in the same place during the summer months. More relevant to the racial profiling controversy, this theory may explain why a Black citizen in a White neighborhood attracts the attention of a police officer *and* why a White citizen in a Black neighborhood attracts the attention of a police officer. Both situations might be equally inconsistent within the contexts of their locations.

Disengagement (De-policing)

Nearly all departments experience reductions in overall productivity when the police are asked (or in some cases required) to collect stop information for a racial profiling study. Disengagement, sometimes referred to as de-policing, occurs as a logical response when police officers become so fearful of being accused of impropriety that they perform at levels substantially less than they should, or worse yet, do nothing at all. Table 10 includes some dramatic examples of overall reductions in police officer productivity that occurred while the officers were collecting stop data during a racial profiling study.

Table 10 – *Reductions in police officer productivity (stops) occurring while the police collect stop information for a racial profiling study.*

Department	Reported percentage reductions in traffic stops or citations issued
Los Angeles, California	25%
Wichita, Kansas	30%
New Jersey (state police)	55%
Minneapolis, Minnesota	63%

Sources: MacDonald 2003; Schultz and Withrow 2004; Withrow 2002

No one really knows why the police report fewer stops during racial profiling studies. Most of the evidence of disengagement is anecdotal, meaning that a few researchers have encountered a few officers who report that they initiate fewer stops during a racial profiling study because they are afraid of being labeled a racist. No empirical or qualitative study has been conducted that connects racial profiling data collection with actual reductions in police productivity. This is likely due to the fact that it is exceedingly difficult to find a comprehensive measure of overall police productivity. Written warnings, citations, arrests, field interviews and other routine police officer activities are typically recorded in separate information systems. In addition, quite a lot of what a police officer does is never recorded anywhere. Furthermore, there are various external factors that are completely unrelated to racial profiling data collection that can and do affect a department's overall productivity. For example, in 2001, the Wichita (Kansas) Police Department reported a 30 percent reduction in stops[2] during the time their officers were collecting racial profiling stop data. At the same time, the City of Wichita experienced a serious budget shortfall and, among other things, eliminated several recruit school sessions, implemented a hiring freeze and greatly reduced allowable overtime. All of these factors resulted in fewer officers on the street, and in turn fewer overall stops. The stops per officer, however, did not change while the department required its officers to collect racial profiling data. In an attempt to follow up on this concern, the department evaluated overall stops during the same period in 2002 when the officers were not required to collect racial profiling data. During this period the overall stops decreased precipitously because an inordinately high number of officers had been called to active military duty following the September 11, 2001 terrorist attacks. Here again, the number of stops per officer remained relatively constant.

The explanation of why police officers report making fewer stops during racial profiling studies is likely influenced by an individual's general attitude toward the police. Supporters of the police may advocate an innocent explanation while critics of the police may be more inclined to support a more insidious motivation. Both types are discussed in the following sections along with some ideas on how to evaluate their potential for explaining a reduction in productivity. While we do not know why police officers report fewer stops during a racial profiling study's data collection period, we do know that such reductions can have a profoundly adverse effect on public safety. The following sections include some examples of how disengagement can threaten a department's overall crime control strategy. Here again, some possible solutions are included.

---

[2] The Wichita Police Department collected racial profiling data from January through July in 2001. During this six-month period the number of stops reported was 30 percent less than the same six-month period in 2000.

A Plausible Explanation

A reduction in police officer productivity during a racial profiling study may be partially related to the time police officers spend filling out stop forms. While it only takes a few moments to complete a standard stop form (either on paper or in an electronic format), collectively these moments add up to a considerable amount of time. While officers are completing stop forms they are not observing traffic and making additional stops.

Second, reductions in police productivity occurring at a time when the police are collecting stop data are more likely explained by inadequate training on which types of stops or police/citizen contacts the police officers are required to report. Most departments do not ask officers to complete a racial profiling stop form during a citizen call for service, while investigating an accident or performing a motorist assist. The common element among these activities is that the police did not initiate the contact, an important aspect of the racial profiling definition. They were either dispatched to the contact or by virtue of their department's policy required to intervene. If a police officer issues a citation during such an event (e.g., following an accident investigation) that citation will not be included in the racial profiling stop data. Collectively, these reporting inconsistencies could result in a perception that the police are making fewer stops, issuing fewer citations or merely not reporting all stops on a racial profiling stop form.

Evaluating these explanations is no easy task because there is no single measure of police productivity. In addition, there is a seemingly endless list of factors, many of which are separate from racial profiling data collection, that affect police officer productivity. Here are a few ideas. First, it is important to consider the validity of the comparative statistic. Productivity during the racial profiling data collection period should be compared to productivity during the same period in the previous year. This will ensure that seasonal variations are taken into account. For example, if the data collection occurred from January through July in 2005, then the comparative period (and statistic) would be from January through July in 2004, and ideally again from January through July in 2006. Second, differences in a department's overall productivity can be explained by changes in patrol strength, usually measured in person hours. If a department experiences a reduction in patrol strength, in either terms of the number of officers working or the number of hours they work, or both, then it should not be surprising that it will also experience a reduction in overall productivity. Fewer officers working fewer hours will initiate fewer stops. Consideration should be given for comparing productivity on a per officer basis. Third, it is important to consider how changes in enforcement strategies and crime patterns, affect a department's overall productivity. For example, if a community experiences an increase in traffic accidents or fatalities caused by excessive speed then a reasonable response from the police department is an increase in speed enforcement (i.e., stops) in selected locations. Similarly, many departments initiate saturation patrol programs in an effort to abate an increase in gang related crime, again, resulting in an overall increase in stops. Conversely, a department may for a number of reasons chose to limit traffic stops and focus its attention on other enforcement strategies, thereby reducing the overall number of stops. The point here is that if any factors are present either during the racial profiling data collection period or within the comparative period that increase or decrease traffic stops then they should be fully accounted for prior to making any conclusions about the possible effect of a racial profiling study on officer productivity. Disengagement is a serious accusation that amounts to nothing less than malfeasance of duty. Such a charge should only be leveled after all possible plausible explanations have been eliminated.

An Insidious Explanation

Critics of the police allege that reductions in police officer productivity are proof of racial profiling. When the police are placed under the glare of public scrutiny, these critics argue, that the police mend their ways and refrain from targeting racial and ethnic minorities thereby explaining the overall reduction of stops. If this explanation is true then the police do a poor job of hiding their alleged transgressions. Despite overall reductions in stops, minority drivers are consistently over-represented in stops.

Second, in preparation for a racial profiling study many departments establish policies requiring officers to report stop information on a standard form. Unfortunately, merely promulgating a rule does not guarantee compliance. Although only documented in one study (Lamberth, 1994), outright deception on the part of the officers responsible for reporting stop information may cause inaccurate stop data, and in some cases, an overall reduction in police officer productivity. There are two forms of such deceptions. *Ghosting* occurs when officers purposely enter the race of the driver incorrectly in order to under report the percentage of minority drivers they actually stop. This practice was documented in 1994, during the New Jersey racial profiling study. In this particular study the officers were required to enter the registration numbers of the cars they stopped. Because New Jersey vehicle records include information on the race of the registered owner, this requirement was considered a means of partially verifying the accuracy of police stop information. The researchers report several incidences whereby officers entered registration numbers from vehicles actually owned and operated by White residents when in actuality they had stopped a vehicle owned and operated by an African-American resident (Meeks 2000). The second type of deception is called balancing. *Balancing* occurs when police officers either chose not to record certain stops, in particular those involving minority drivers, or establish differential enforcement criteria based on race or ethnicity whereby minority drivers are less likely to be stopped than non-minority drivers. A simpler form of balancing may occur when officers wait until the end of a shift to fill out the race or ethnicity of the drivers they stop and merely report percentages similar to what they believe the estimate of the driving population (i.e., the benchmark) suggests they should be stopping.

There are three strategies for addressing de-policing.

First, as is true with other forms of officer deception and/or misbehavior, active supervision is an effective tool. Much of police work is conducted well out of sight of active supervision. This does not necessarily mean that a conscientious supervisor would not be able to detect deception. In fact, attentive patrol supervisors are in the best position to uncover evidence of officer misconduct.

Second, internal audit systems are quite effective at reducing the potential for deception. The most effective audit systems tie police stop reports to actual persons. For example, if the officers are required to include the driver's license number of the person they stop then (assuming the driver's license record actually includes the licensee's race or ethnicity) an audit could easily identify an erroneous record. Such a system would be particularly useful if an actual citation, arrest or police case were generated and the information from that is tied to the police stop record. Although time consuming, routine spot checks of video records may provide some insight into the veracity of police stop records.

Finally, it appears that behavioral changes cannot be sustained over the long haul. Deception can only last so long before it is detected. The longer a data collection lasts the less likely deceptive behaviors can be sustained.

Disengagement and Its Effect on Public Safety

In 1982, James Q. Wilson and George Kelling published *Broken Windows*, arguably one of the most influential articles on policing philosophy in the last century. In this article Wilson and Kelling effectively argue that police officers inattentiveness to minor indiscretions (e.g., panhandling, fare beating and other minor public disorder crimes) leads to more serious criminal behaviors. Using the analogy of an untended broken window in an abandoned building they propose that if the window is not quickly repaired then future passersby will be encouraged to break more windows until there are no solid panes of glass left. It is after all, quite amusing to break a window with a rock. If, however, the window is repaired then passersby will assume somebody cares enough to respond to this minor indiscretion and, more importantly, that somebody may confront them when they attempt to break another window.

Over the past two decades countless tests have confirmed Wilson and Kelling's *Broken Windows* proposition. When the police fail to respond to minor crime and public disorder then future criminals will be emboldened to commit more serious violations. Herein is the danger associated with officer disengagement related to the racial profiling controversy. If the police disengage out of fear that an analysis of their legitimately initiated traffic stops will be considered evidence of their racist motivations then a police officer, or several officers, may simply chose not to confront minor traffic violations.

Such occurrences have already been documented anecdotally in two large cities. In one city the police classify potential stops involving minority drivers as NCNC or No Contact, No Complaint stops. In this case police officers appear to avoid either making a lot of stops in neighborhoods populated primarily by racial and ethnic minorities and/or knowingly refrain from stopping racial or ethnic minorities. The officers in another city have a more colorful name for such stops – FIDO, or Fuck It, Drive On stops. The result is the same. Some police officers in these communities are actively ignoring violations committed by racial and ethnic minorities in order to avoid the possibility that their stops will be considered racially motivated.

This story (actually happened) illustrates the paradox of officer disengagement within the context of the racial profiling controversy. Following the publication of a racial profiling study in a mid-sized Midwestern community the president of the local NAACP chapter actually asked the chief of police to reduce the number of police officers assigned to the predominantly African-American parts of town. This, he argued, would reduce the overall number of African-American residents who are arrested by the police. Of course, the chapter president is correct. In this particular community these neighborhoods also have high crime rates. If the police are not assigned to work there then the number of arrests that might arise from routine patrol would decrease. Before the chief of police could respond another citizen, who happens to live in one of the high crime beats, stood up and quite convincingly urged the chapter president to "mind your own ... business." "If the cops stop coming to Midtown then the gangs will take over. We was the ones who convinced the police to come down there more often ten years ago when we had a lot of drive-bys. No, chief, you keep them police coming. We like them down here."

5
How to Win a Court Challenge

Some legal issues within the racial profiling controversy are settled. A police officer cannot use the race of the driver alone as a means to initiate a traffic stop (*United States v. Brignoni-Ponce*, 1975; *United States v. Jones*, 2001). A police officer may use the race of the driver in combination with other identifying factors (e.g., a physical description of a known criminal suspect) to initiate a stop (*Brown v. City of Oneonta*, 2000; *United States v. Martinez-Fuente*, 1976; *United States v. Montero-Camaro*, 2000). A police officer may not use a suspect's race alone as a basis for conducting a consent interview or search (*United States v. Travis*, 1995).

The leading racial profiling case is *Whren et al. v. United States*. Decided in 1996, this case heightened our awareness of the potential for certain police procedures, namely pretextual stops, to result in the disparate treatment of minorities. Here are the facts. On the evening of June 10, 1993, two plainclothes detectives from the District of Columbia Metropolitan Police Department were patrolling a high crime and drug area in an unmarked car. They became suspicious of two youthful occupants in a Nissan Pathfinder waiting at a stop sign for what seemed like an unusually long time. The officers had previously observed these individuals leaving a known crack house. When the detectives turned around to follow the car the driver turned without signaling and sped off at an unreasonable speed. The detectives overtook the Pathfinder at the next stop light, identified themselves and asked the driver to pull over to the curb. As one of the detectives approached the Pathfinder he noticed two large plastic bags of what appeared to be crack cocaine in the passenger's hands. The occupants were arrested, charged and ultimately convicted of various federal drug laws.

The defendants attempted to suppress the evidence at a pre-trial hearing by alleging that the detectives did not have probable cause that the defendants were engaged in illegal drug activity. More specifically they alleged that the detectives' decision to initiate the stop (based on a traffic violation) was merely a pretext for conducting a more invasive search or investigation into possible drug trafficking. The detectives agreed that the stop for a traffic violation was in fact pretextual; however, by virtue of their authority, they were legally authorized to stop a motorist for violating the traffic law. Furthermore, they argued that the results of a legal search (in this case based on plain view) should not be suppressed if the initial stop (for the traffic violation) is legal. The trial court agreed and admitted the evidence. The Court of Appeals affirmed the convictions, holding with respect to the suppression issue that, "regardless of whether a police officer subjectively believes that the occupants of an automobile may be engaging in some other illegal behavior, a traffic stop is permissible as long as a reasonable officer in the same circumstances could have stopped the car for the suspected traffic violation." A unanimous Supreme Court agreed and upheld the convictions.

The *Whren* decision did not create the pretextual stop. Indeed, the pretextual stop has been an effective crime detection and suppression tool for decades. It is perfectly legal for a police officer to initiate a traffic stop on observing a bona fide violation of the law. If events and conditions during the stop justify (legal and otherwise) a more thorough investigation and/or search then, assuming the suspect's rights are not subsequently violated, any evidence arising from this stop is admissible. The *Whren* decision did not, as has been suggested by some experts (see, for example, Barlow and Barlow 2002; Harris 1997 and 2002; Jernigan 2000), change the direction of search and seizure jurisprudence. In fact, the *Whren* decision is quite consistent with nearly fifty years of legal precedent.

The racial profiling controversy has produced a new legal avenue for plaintiffs seeking relief from prosecution and a platform for advocacy groups to advertise their displeasure with the police. Although several important cases have been decided and a pattern is emerging, it is too early to determine which statute or legal precedent will become the primary basis for racial profiling related litigation. The possible legal avenues of racial profiling related legal challenges are discussed and evaluated in this chapter. A common pattern has emerged on how plaintiff's attorneys build and argue racial profiling cases. This pattern is revealed in this chapter and several suggestions are offered on how police departments can effectively defend themselves. The final section outlines the legal strategies that have worked, not worked and might work in the future. It is highly likely that the Obama Administration will focus more attention and resources on the racial profiling controversy. In doing so, it is likely that the same legal strategy that produced the ten-year consent decree against the New Jersey State Police will be resurrected.

Possible Sources of Legal Challenges

The first major racial profiling studies (e.g., New Jersey and Maryland) actually originated from legal challenges and were commissioned by court orders. This practice continues today, however, the most common route to the courthouse is a legal challenge encouraged by an independently commissioned study. For example, in 2003, the Police Foundation conducted a statewide racial profiling study in Kansas. This study finds (albeit erroneously) that "racial profiling is occurring throughout the State of Kansas." Following the publication of the study four defendants who had been previously stopped, searched (by consent), arrested and then charged with drug possession filed pretrial motions to suppress the evidence. These defendants were stopped on the interstate highway. The basis of their motions was that they were racially profiled (i.e., stopped because they are racial or ethnic minorities) and the Police Foundation's report provided support for their argument. If true, the police officers would have violated the defendants' rights to due process and equal protection. A finding in their favor would have suppressed the evidence under the fruit of the poisonous tree doctrine and then a likely dismissal of the drug charges. Eventually these motions to suppress were heard by three federal District Court judges in Topeka Kansas. Almost immediately the validity and reliability of the Police Foundation study's methodology became an issue. Various experts (including the author) and statisticians were called to testify. Ultimately, none of these motions to suppress were successful and all four defendants were convicted.

The central issue of these legal challenges is whether the police enforced the law equally or whether a portion of our society, namely racial and ethnic minorities, must endure a special disadvantage under the law. Generally, the cases that are related to a criminal proceeding (usually involving a traffic stop) are based on some derivative of the Fourth, Fifth and Fourteenth Amendments to the United States Constitution. Civil cases tend to be based on Section 42, U.S.C., Section 14141 and could possibly be based on Section 42, U.S.C, Section 1983. Although 27 states now have statutes prohibiting racial profiling, litigation at the state level is rather sparse and inconsistent. The following table provides an evaluation on the viability of these legal options in racial profiling litigation (see Table 11).

Table 11 – *Viability of various legal options in racial profiling litigation.*

Source of Law/ Basis of Legal Argument	Description	History	Potential Viability
Fourth Amendment	"No warrant shall issue, but on probable cause, supported by Oath or affirmation, and particularly describing the place to be searched, and the persons of things to be searched."	Original source of law regulating search and seizure in American policing. There are several exceptions to the warrant rule, namely the consent search, that are highly relevant to the racial profiling controversy.	*Whren* effectively closed the door to racial profiling decisions based on the Fourth Amendment by allowing police officers to apply an objective rather than a subjective test when initiating a traffic stop. Most racial profiling cases that include a Fourth Amendment argument focus on the legality of the actual search rather than the race of the defendant.
Fifth and Fourteenth Amendments (due process clause)	"No state shall make or enforce any law which shall abridge the privileges of immunities of citizens of the United States; nor shall any State deprive any person of life, liberty, or property, without due process of law; nor deny to any person within its jurisdiction the equal protection of the laws."	The Fifth Amendment is the origin of due process in American law. The Fourteenth was ratified after the Civil War to insure that all citizens (regardless of which state they happen to live in) enjoy the same level of Constitutional protections, i.e., equal protection under the law.	The *Whren* court said the Fourteenth would be an effective remedy if the plaintiff could prove both a discriminatory effect and a discriminatory intent on the part of the police officers. The plaintiff must prove that he was subjected to selective enforcement. This can only be done if the plaintiff

Source of Law/ Basis of Legal Argument	Description	History	Potential Viability
Fifth and Fourteenth Amendments (due process clause) *Continued*			can prove that similarly situated individuals who are not racial or ethnic minorities could have been but were not stopped.
Title 42, U.S.C., Section 14141	"Unlawful for any governmental authority, or agent thereof, or any person acting on behalf of a government authority, to engage in a pattern or practice of conduct by law enforcement officers or by officials or employees of any governmental agency with responsibility for the administration of juvenile justice or the incarceration of juveniles that deprives persons of rights, privileges, or immunities secured or protected by the constitution or laws of the United States."	This provision was part of the Crime Control Act of 1994. Only the United States Attorney General has the authority to file a case under this section. The law is designed to address patterns and practices of abuse. This statute has been effective in various cases involving excessive force, harassment, false arrest, coercive sexual conduct and unlawful searches and seizures.	This provision was used quite effectively in the case that led to the acceptance of a consent decree by the New Jersey State Police. These cases focus on the entire pattern and practice of a department's enforcement program. There is no need for an individual defendant. Although the law does not provide for punitive damages, losing such a challenge can have a profound effect on a department's routine operations.

Source of Law/ Basis of Legal Argument	Description	History	Potential Viability
Title 42, U.S.C., Section 1983	Every person who under cover of any statute, ordinance, regulation, custom, or usage, of any State or Territory or the District of Columbia, subjects, or causes to be subjected, any citizen of the United States or other person within the jurisdiction thereof to the deprivation of any rights, privileges, or immunities secured by the Constitution and laws, shall be liable to the party injured in an action at law, Suit in equity, or other proper proceeding for redress, except that in any action brought against a judicial officer for an act or omission taken in such officer's judicial capacity, injunctive relief shall not be granted unless a declaratory decree was violated or declaratory relief was unavailable.	Part of the Civil Rights Act of 1871. This law was designed to deter state governments from passing laws that discriminated against former slaves. Section 1983 provides a mechanism for aggrieved parties to seek relief from state actors (e.g., the police) for abuse conducted within their official capacities.	This statute could be an effective remedy in a racial profiling case if the plaintiff could prove 1) that the stop was predicated on race alone, and 2) that he was substantially harmed because of the stop. Neither of these are easy to prove, given the quality of racial profiling research data. Also, it is unlikely that the plaintiff will be able to prove that the officer acted within his "official capacity" because a police department is not likely to have a policy encouraging its officers to engage in racial profiling. Ultimately, the viability of this legal remedy is hampered by the costs associated with collecting the evidence and the monetary limits place on damages.
State level statutes that prohibit racial profiling	These are variously worded. Most only prohibit racial profiling (defined conceptually) or require departments to collect stop information. Very few of these statutes proscribe a legal remedy.	These statutes became popular in the late 1990s. To date, 27 states have some type of racial profiling statute. In some cases these provisions are merely resolutions and/or provide no penalty rendering them rather useless as a legal remedy.	Most of these statutes require the plaintiff to prove that the police officer initiated the stop because of the plaintiff's race or ethnicity. As has been previously demonstrated, this is a very difficult allegation to prove.

Regardless of the actual legal basis of their claims, there are two common challenges facing plaintiffs in racial profiling cases.

First, plaintiffs experience considerable difficulty proving that the police officer stopped them because of their race or ethnicity. It is quite difficult, and maybe impossible, to prove that a police officer was actually aware of the plaintiff's race or ethnicity prior to the stop *and* that the police officer based his decision to initiate the stop on this reason alone.

Second, the quality of racial profiling data, namely the benchmarks, is not sufficient enough to determine whether certain racial or ethnic groups are more or less likely to be stopped. We simply have not found a way to measure the racial or ethnic proportions of the population of individuals who could or should be stopped but are actually not stopped. Unless and until an accurate benchmarking method is established, court challenges that attempt to prove a disparate effect will not likely be very successful.

How Plaintiff's Attorneys Build Racial Profiling Cases

As previously mentioned, there are two varieties of racial profiling cases. The first and most common, involve a single criminal defendant alleging that the traffic stop that produced the evidence to be used against him in a criminal proceeding was discriminatory. These allegations tend to arise in pretrial motions to suppress evidence based on a claim that the stop violated the defendant's Constitutional rights, usually equal protection. If successful, under the exclusionary rule and fruits of the poisonous tree doctrine, any evidence arising from an unconstitutional stop would be inadmissible in a subsequent criminal proceeding. The second type of case is usually civil and may even be a class action. In these cases, which are quite rare, the plaintiffs attempt to prove that the police department's overall enforcement patterns and practices have a discriminatory effect. To be successful the plaintiff would have to prove that the members of certain racial or ethnic groups are more at risk of being stopped by the police.

Individual Cases Arising Out of Criminal Proceedings

The central issue in these cases is whether the police officer who initiated the stop did so because of the defendant's race or ethnicity. *To be successful the defendant must prove that 1) the police officer knew the defendant's race or ethnicity prior to the stop, and 2) the police officer initiated the stop based on a false assumption that members of the defendant's racial or ethnic group are more likely to be guilty of serious crimes.* In other words, the defendant must prove that he was racially profiled by that particular officer.

Unless the defendant has direct evidence that the police officer knew the driver's race and then initiated the stop because of it then it is not likely that the court will rule in the defendant's favor. Of course, direct evidence of this sort, if it exists at all, resides only in the mind of the police officer.

In most cases, defendants' attorneys are forced to base their arguments on one of the following indirect arguments.

- **People like my client are more at risk of being stopped by the police.**

Evaluating the truth of this allegation is deceptively simple. You only have to know two things:

First, you need to know how many people like the attorney's client are stopped by the police. This information is often readily available from a recent racial profiling study conducted in the same jurisdiction where the stop occurred. Absent that the defendant's attorney can review police stop, arrest or booking data.

Second, you need to know how many people like the attorney's client are available to be stopped. The description "available to be stopped" has multiple meanings.

For example, does this mean the percentage of all drivers in the community who are like the attorney's client, those who violate the law, those who are observed by a police officer, or those who violate the law while being observed by a police officer? This is not a flippant question. To evaluate the probability of anything, you must divide the number of actual outcomes (in this case the number of individuals like the defendant who are stopped) by the total number of possible outcomes (in this case the total number of individuals like the defendant who are not stopped). Here again, the elusive denominator thwarts defendants as much as it does researchers.

The description "like my client" also has multiple meanings. Most observers think this means somebody of the same race or ethnic group. It is more complicated than that. "Like" also means "similar" and the legal concept is **similarly situated**. A more precisely stated allegation would be, "Individuals who are similarly situated with my client (meaning observed by a police officer in the same place, at the same time, doing the same thing, etc.) are more likely to be stopped if they are members of the same race or ethnic group as my client." This is akin to the "all things being equal" argument alleging that if two drivers are observed committing the same violation at the same time by the same officer, which one would be stopped? Of course the obvious answer is the first driver who pulls over after the officer turns on his lights. As ridiculous as this seems, the similarly situated concept illustrates the contextual and dynamic nature of routine patrol operations. Of course, no two situations can be exactly the same. Routine police work is contextual and the decisions made by police officers are highly influenced by what is happening at the time they observe a violation. When you ask a seasoned police officer, "What would you do if...?" you are likely to get a response, "Well, it depends on...." Police officers do not make decisions in a laboratory or under experimental conditions. Defendants alleging they are stopped because of their race are required to demonstrate that the police officer tends to stop individuals of the same race even though individuals of a different race are observed doing the same thing, a near impossible task.

Another meaning of "like my client" implies **selective enforcement**. This allegation is based on the notion that racial and ethnic minorities are more likely to be stopped for less serious violations than non-minorities. In other words, the enforcement tolerance for racial and ethnic minorities is narrower than for non-minorities, thereby placing minorities more at risk of being stopped. For example, some defendant's attorneys will allege that the police are quick to stop a Black driver for a minor traffic infraction while looking the other way when they observe a White driver committing a more serious violation. Of course, to prove this allegation the defendant's attorney must present evidence that the officer was actually aware of the driver's race or ethnicity prior to the stop, which is not likely. Defendants' attorneys making such allegations are further challenged by the stop data. Many stop data sets include a variable describing the reason for the stop. Unfortunately, the attributes of this variable do not describe the relative severity of the driver's behavior prior to the stop. For example, an officer may report that two of the drivers he stopped were stopped for a "speeding" violation. One driver could have been stopped in an occupied school zone and the other on a sparsely traveled interstate highway. Both are "speeding" violations; however, they are quite different in terms of their severity and threat to public safety. In short, it is unlikely that a defendant's attorney will have detailed enough stop data to prove that racial and ethnic minorities are stopped for less serious violations.

Finally, this allegation is based on a common, but serious, logical error called an ecological fallacy. An **ecological fallacy** occurs when one assumes that individual behavior can be predicted by group behavior. For example, Roman Catholicism is the predominant religious preference in Mexico. My wife and I have invited some Mexican friends of ours over to dinner on a Friday evening during Lent. We decide to serve fish because we assume our friends are Roman Catholic. In other words, we've predicted our friends' religious preference based on what we know about a large group of people who are similar to them. Regardless of whether or not we predicted accurately, we've committed an ecological fallacy. The same thing occurs when a racial profiling study (encompassing an entire department) is used as proof that an individual police officer within that department engaged in racial profiling when he stopped an individual driver. What happens at the aggregate or group level is in no way indicative of what might have happened at the individual level. Even if the department-wide racial profiling study definitively concludes (albeit unlikely) that individuals like the defendant are more at risk of being stopped by the police, this does not necessarily mean that this officer racially profiled this defendant.

- **People like my client are more at risk of being stopped by this officer.**

In this case the focus of the allegation is on the individual officer. In effect, the defendant's attorney is attempting to prove that the officer is a racist in an effort to diminish the officer's credibility in the eyes of the judge or jury. Of course, there is no definitive test that can determine whether or not a person is actually a racist. There are a few tests available that claim to measure an individual's "racist tendency," however, none are proven to be valid or even reliable. Most are little more than self-inventory tests like the "feel good" test found in popular magazines. Besides, even if such a test existed and an officer subjecting himself to it found out that he has racist tendencies that does not necessarily mean that the officer behaved in accordance with these tendencies while making this stop. The relationship between attitudes, even unconscious attitudes, and behavior is tenuous at best.

What the defendant's attorney will attempt to do is prove that this officer tends to stop an over-representation of racial minorities. The defendant's attorney will attempt to secure information (i.e., race, ethnicity, age, reason, etc.) about the individuals stopped by the officer. So what if he does? Without an accurate benchmark or estimate of the population (broken down by race and ethnicity) of the individuals actually observed and not stopped by this officer, it is not possible to use stop information as proof of an officer's alleged discriminatory behavior.

In addition, the defendant's attorney will have two additional challenges while attempting to use this information.

First, who a police officer stops is largely dependent on where the officer is assigned to work. It is quite common in racial profiling studies conducted in urban settings to find several officers who stop nearly exclusively racial or ethnic minorities. Nearly every time on closer examination the analyst will find that these officers are assigned to work in beats and neighborhoods that are populated primarily by the same racial or ethnic minorities. It should come as no surprise that when an officer is assigned to work in a part of town that is populated principally by a particular racial or ethnic group that the stops made by that officer tend to involve individuals of the same racial or ethnic groups.

Second, a typical stop data set records the race and/or ethnicity of individuals *after* they are stopped, not before. Knowledge about the race and/or ethnicity of a driver measured after they are stopped is purely academic. The critical factor here, again, is the officer's perception of the driver's race and/or ethnicity *prior* to the stop.

A more sophisticated defendant's attorney may attempt to obtain the stop records of all similarly situated officers. In this case the defendant's attorney will compare the performance of the officer who stopped his client with the performances of other officers who work in the same place or time and enforced the same law. For example, if the defendant was stopped by a generally assigned patrol officer in the evening within the confines of a well-defined neighborhood, the defendant's attorney will compare this officer's stops (by the race and ethnicity of the drivers stopped) with officers who are also generally assigned patrol duty in the same beat during roughly the same time frame. In doing so, the defendant's attorney is attempting to create an internal benchmark. If the officer who stopped the defendant tends to stop a statistically significantly higher proportion of individuals of the same race or ethnicity as the defendant, when compared to this officer's similarly situated work peers, then this might suggest that this officer's behavior has a disparate impact on racial or ethnic minorities. The key objective in defending this allegation is to focus on how the defendant's attorney defines "similarly situated."

> **Even though police officers are generally assigned to patrol duties within the same beat and shift does not necessarily mean that they:**
>
> *1. perform the same duties, and*
>
> *2. observe the same population of drivers.*

Often officers are regularly but temporarily assigned to perform specific tasks that other officers working in the same area are not asked or capable of doing. For example, during an informal analysis of stop data in a small community the author identified an officer who reported stopping an inordinately high percentage of Hispanic drivers. Upon further investigation the author learned that this is the only officer in the department who speaks Spanish. When non-Spanish-speaking officers stop Spanish-speaking drivers they routinely refer the stop to this Spanish-speaking officer. This officer reports the stop as his own per a general agreement with his work peers.

Further complicating this patrol beats are seldom homogenous with respect to traffic patterns and the race and ethnicity of their driving populations. Most beats contain residential, commercial, retail and mixed-use areas. Officers assigned to the same beat same shift may work primarily in very different locations. In short, unless the stop data include variables that properly document every possible contingency that may affect how, when, where and why officers work (and none so far have), it is likely not possible to determine which officers are "similarly assigned." This problem is further exacerbated when officers are dispersed throughout a large geographic area, such as, in a rural policing or highway patrol context.

Civil Cases Involving Groups

Racial profiling litigation involving groups or classes of individuals often alleges that a department's overall enforcement program is either intentionally or unintentionally discriminatory against a protected class of individuals. These cases base their arguments on various statutes and legal concepts, including Title 42, U.S.C., Section 14141 (Pattern and Practice) or Equal Protection. The evidence used to support these allegations is really no different from that used in a case involving an individual. The population of individuals (by race and ethnicity) stopped by the police is compared to the population of individuals (by race and ethnicity) at risk of being stopped. *Beyond this there are two important issues that warrant attention.*

- **Racial profiling cases involving groups are structurally similar to affirmative action cases.**

In an affirmative action case the plaintiff is not required to prove intentional discrimination. A simple comparison of the population of individuals (by race and ethnicity) who applied for the job with the population of individuals (by race and ethnicity) who were actually offered employment revealing a disparate effect is enough to establish *prima facie* evidence of discrimination. For example, if ten percent of the people who applied for a job are African-American but only one percent of the individuals who are offered a job are African-American then a court may conclude that the employment process is discriminatory. Of course, the plaintiffs in an affirmative action case have a substantial advantage over racial profiling researchers. They have an accurate measure of the group of individuals who are likely to be selected for a job. Human resources departments routinely collect demographic information (e.g., race, ethnicity, gender, age, veteran status) about the individuals who apply for jobs. Unlike racial profiling researchers who must rely on benchmark estimates, affirmative action plaintiffs have a valid and reliable measure of the population available for employment.

- **Racial profiling cases involving groups avoid an ecological fallacy.**

Many racial profiling cases involving individuals attempt to use aggregate data (e.g., in the form of a citywide racial profiling study) as proof that the officer that stopped them was discriminatory. As mentioned previously, this is an ecological fallacy. It is not possible to use information collected from groups as proof of individual motivation. Cases involving groups avoid this because the issue is precisely the effect of the enforcement program on the entire protected class of individuals.

The previously discussed strategies for successfully defending oneself or a department against an individual racial profiling allegation are useful in a class action case. Many of these become more important and one is irrelevant in a class action case.

During a class action allegation:
– *The benchmark estimate of the driving population (i.e., the population at risk of being stopped) is more important.* Defendants are generally more successful when they are able to demonstrate to the court that the benchmark is either an invalid or unreliable measure of either the overall driving

population or, better yet, the population of individuals actually at risk of being stopped by the police.

– The manner in which the police department deploys patrol resources is more significant. Cities are not homogenous social institutions. Crime rates and levels of victimization vary between neighborhoods, beats and patrol districts. Policing leaders tend to assign more resources to the parts of town that experience higher crime rates, levels of victimization and more citizen calls for service. Sometimes these parts of town are populated primarily by racial and ethnic minorities. When more policing resources are legitimately assigned to these parts of town then it may appear that overall the police are targeting racial minorities. As a result, defending a class action litigation requires a beat level analysis of police stop data demonstrating that policing resources are legitimately assigned to the parts of town that need them and how this might affect the overall enforcement program.

– The reason for the stops becomes more relevant. It is likely that a class action plaintiff will allege that racial or ethnic minorities are stopped more frequently for relatively minor offenses. Given the nondescript nature in which this variable is measured it is not likely that the plaintiff will be able to support this allegation. For example, stops for "speeding" can be as serious as five miles over the limit in a school zone or as innocuous as five miles over the limit in on a rural highway. Stops for "equipment violations" can be as serious as an inoperable headlight at night or as benign as a dirty license plate. In short, in most police stop data sets it is not really possible to determine how serious the drivers' behaviors are prior to the stop.

– The result of the stops will be used to allege further disparate treatment. Differences between racial and ethnic groups with respect to arrests and searches will be used as evidence that the police are discriminatory. Often a more thorough analysis reveals that arrests are based on non-discretionary factors, like warrants. Also, departments are in a better defensive position when they are able to demonstrate that most of their arrests actually result in the filing of a criminal charge. Searches should also be evaluated separately

with respect to their motivation and level of discretion. Searches predicated on a lawful arrest or for inventory purposes are often required by law or policy. Unlike consent searches these are non-discretionary and should not be considered potentially discriminatory.

– *The officer's intent or motivation for initiating the traffic stop is irrelevant in a class action lawsuit.* An individual alleging racial profiling must prove that the officer was aware of the plaintiff's race prior to the stop and initiated the stop based primarily on this information, as opposed to the plaintiff's actual behavior. In other words, the plaintiff must prove that the officer actually intended to discriminate based on race or ethnicity. In a class action case, the officers' intent is irrelevant. During a class action allegation, the overall (allegedly disparate) effect of the department's enforcement practices is important. In other words, in a class action lawsuit it really does not matter who the officers *intended* to stop. What matters is who the officers *actually* stopped.

Legal Strategies That Have Worked, Not Worked and Might Work

What "works" really depends on which side of the court-room you sit. For the purposes of this section, let us assume that by "works" I mean the strategies that have been successfully used by litigants who allege racial profiling.

What's Worked

The two most successful and far-reaching racial profiling lawsuits occurred early in the controversy in New Jersey and Maryland. Both cases resulted in the acceptance of comprehensive consent decrees that, until recently, have constrained the departments involved in unprecedented ways.

In both cases, several factors affected the outcome in favor of the plaintiffs alleging racial profiling.

First, because these occurred early in the controversy, there was really no body of literature within which to evaluate the validity of the study's methods. The researcher relied on a field observation benchmark, a procedure he invented. As mentioned in a previous chapter, the validity and reliability of the benchmarks (estimates of the driving population) produced by this strategy is highly questionable. At the time of these lawsuits, however, this benchmarking strategy had not been subjected to rigorous testing. In effect, this was the only game in town.

Second, in the absence of an effective counter argument (provided by an expert witness for the defense) the plaintiff's expert was able to convince the court that his conclusions were definitive. The racial profiling controversy had not yet matured to the point where it had attracted the attention of competent researchers who had a better understanding of routine police systems and practices. The plaintiff's expert was, in effect, the only credible perspective the court heard. Subsequent cases wherein more informed expert witnesses were used have effectively discredited this particular research methodology.

Finally, the plaintiff was able to produce evidence beyond the statistics that demonstrated a discriminatory intent on the part of the defendants. The researcher's review of documents, policies, directives, letters, e-mails, training reports and other similar items produced evidence that the defendant intended to target racial and ethnic minorities in their desire to increase drug interdiction.

What's Not Worked

Subsequent racial profiling litigations have been less than successful for plaintiffs. The emerging racial profiling controversy attracted a great deal of attention and produced a number of credible researchers who are willing to consider the evidence from a more objective perspective. As a result, plaintiffs are less able to present incontrovertible evidence suggesting that racial and ethnic minorities are more likely to be stopped, searched or arrested.

Here are a few of the strategies that have not worked for plaintiffs.

–*Plaintiffs continue to use benchmark estimates of the driving population that are well known to be unreliable and invalid.* Unless and until plaintiffs can find benchmarks that accurately and reliably measure the overall driving population (or the population at risk of being stopped) then it is not possible for them to allege that the police stop a disproportionately high proportion of racial and ethnic minorities. To the extent defendants are successful at demonstrating the measurement error associated with these benchmarks they are successful in court. Normally, this requires the assistance of an individual trained in statistical analysis and knowledgeable about routine police systems and practices.

–*For the most part, plaintiffs pay little attention to routine police operations.* They do so at their own peril. For example, many plaintiffs assume searches are basically the same. The fact is, searches and particularly the justification for searches vary widely. Some searches are required by law or policy (incident to arrest, inventory) while others are highly discretionary (consent). The most important distinction between searches is the level of officer discretion. Unfortunately many plaintiffs either do not analyze searches by type or merely fail to understand the differences between them.

–*The available data are insufficient and provide considerable opportunities for defendants to raise reasonable doubt.* Police stop data are seldom able to capture important nuances existing within the contexts of stops that often explain why a police officer behaved in the way he did. For example, sometimes plaintiffs attempt to associate the reason for a stop with the outcome of a stop. The objective of this exercise is to see if racial and ethnic minorities are either stopped for less serious violations or to determine whether racial and ethnic minorities when stopped are more likely to get cited or arrested for offenses that non-minorities get warned for. Unfortunately, the reason for the stop in most stop data sets is only nominally measured and thus cannot be organized into a logical order of seriousness. Most departments merely report the reason as a "traffic violation," "equipment violation," or "other violation." Within each of these categories there is considerable variation with respect to the seriousness of the driver's behavior leading to the stop.

–*Most individual plaintiffs are unsuccessful because they attempt to use department wide studies as evidence that the officer who stopped them was discriminatory.* Such thinking is a serious logical mistake called an ecological fallacy.

Aggregate level data can neither prove nor disprove an individual officer's motivation for initiating a traffic stop.

–Most plaintiffs are unable to produce evidence that the officer actually intended to stop the defendant because of the defendant's race or ethnicity. The race or ethnicity of drivers stopped is normally collected after the stop, not before. As a result there is really no way for a plaintiff to allege that the officer actually knew the defendant's race prior to the stop, much less used this information inappropriately as justification for the stop. Furthermore, most plaintiffs are unable to locate evidence (e.g., letters, e-mails, other documents) that the officer harbors racist attitudes. This would be analogous to a district attorney developing evidence that a defendant intended to commit a particular offense based on the defendant's prior behaviors. The lack of such evidence is likely due to the fact that very few police officers harbor racist attitudes and those that might seldom share such feelings and/or express them in public.

–The rules of causality are unknown to most plaintiffs. To prove that one thing is the cause of another (e.g., that being a racial minority is the cause of being stopped) a researcher must prove all three causal rules—temporal order, correlation, lack of plausible alternative explanations. These rules and how they function in a racial profiling context are discussed in a previous chapter. In the end, plaintiffs are seldom able to prove that a driver's race is a cause for a police officer's decision to initiate a traffic stop.

What Might Work

Some "experts" have come to the conclusion that we may never be able to actually prove racial profiling. Such definitive statements seldom prove accurate over time. Eventually, a method will emerge that will produce the data necessary to definitively prove that an individual or group of individuals are being racially profiled, assuming, of course, they actually are being profiled.

In the interim, some promising strategies are emerging.
–The use of an operational definition effectively makes proving racial profiling easier. Operational definitions merely

allege that an over-representation of racial minorities in police stops is enough to prove racial profiling. Research based on this definition is more likely to produce a finding of racial profiling. Research based on a conceptual definition is seldom likely to conclude that racial profiling is occurring. Conceptual definitions require the accuser to actually prove that the police 1) knew the driver's race or ethnicity prior to the stop, and 2) acted inappropriately on this information to initiate the stop. Of course both definitions rely heavily on an accurate estimate of the population of drivers that are not stopped— something that has so far eluded racial profiling researchers.

–The use of internal benchmarks may overcome many of the problems caused by using aggregate data (i.e., department-wide stop studies) as evidence of individual discriminatory intent. Internal benchmarks (described in an earlier chapter) are an effective technique for identifying and controlling errant police officer behavior. They are used in departments that have had a history of police abuse. When properly constructed (and this is no easy feat) an internal benchmark could provide insight into an individual officer's behavior within the context of his or her similarly situated peers.

6

The Importance of Enforcing the Whole Law

S tate traffic codes and municipal ordinances describe thousands of situations that when observed by police officers produce the probable cause necessary to initiate a legal traffic stop. Stops predicated on a bona fide violation of the law are legal and, according to the decision in *Whren*; searches, arrests and other stop events emanating from them are also legal. This means that, unless the police subsequently violate an individual's Constitutional rights during a legal stop, any evidence obtained is admissible and any arrest is lawful. In effect, traffic codes and municipal ordinances provide thousands of probable cause generating events.

Such discretionary authority is an important issue in the racial profiling controversy. Critics of the police allege that the police will merely use benign traffic statutes (e.g., a dirty license plate) as a pretext for initiating the stop of a person they are interested in searching, but have no legal justification for doing so. In fact, this is precisely what happened in *Whren*, the leading racial profiling case. The officers that initiated the stop in *Whren* were assigned to the vice squad, not the sort of enforcement assignment that relies heavily on traffic stops. The officers suspected Whren and his companion were in possession of a controlled substance because they had observed them leaving a house well known as a place where drugs are bought and sold. They attempted no subterfuge. They did not have to. The stop for the traffic violation (failure to signal a lane change) was legal. Therefore the subsequent plain view search that produced the contraband was also legal. Proponents of the police consider the decision in *Whren* to be a validation of a long standing and important policing strategy.

This does not, however, mean that the police can rely on *Whren* with impunity. As is often the case when a procedure is overused or when the philosophy of the appellate court system changes, the police often find themselves in a difficult position. It took decades for the police to fully implement the far-reaching decisions handed down by the Warren Court during the 1960s. One can only imagine how routine police procedures would change should the *Whren* decision be overturned.

The purpose of this chapter is to recommend the judicious use of the traffic code as an important part of a comprehensive enforcement or drug interdiction policy. The objective here is to encourage the police to use, but not overuse, the law so as to avoid a potential racial profiling problem.

The Popularity Trap

In business there is an old adage called the 80/20 rule. This rule proposes that 80 percent of any business's activity is produced by 20 percent of its customers. In criminal justice, we have a similar rule. We say that 90 percent of the crime is committed by 10 percent of the population. A corollary to this rule may be that 90 percent of the traffic stops are for the same reason—likely a speeding violation. A police department reporting that a majority of the stops made by its officers are for speed violations would not be at all surprising. Speeding is a serious threat to public safety. Most accidents are caused by drivers who drive too fast. Speed violations are easily quantifiable. If the driver is operating a vehicle faster than the posted speed limit then an objective violation has occurred. There is seldom little need to prove intent or knowledge. Speeding violations are easy.

What Makes Some Violations "Popular"?
Beyond speeding, some violations become popular; that is, they are often used among officers.

There are at least five reasons for the popularity of a particular violation:
– *Where an officer is assigned often determines the types of violations he will encounter and enforce.* Officers assigned to high volume expressways tend to observe a lot of speeding violations. Officers assigned to entertainment or restaurant districts may observe a higher proportion of parking or pedestrian violations.

– What an officer is assigned to do sometimes determines the types of violations he enforces. Officers assigned as school resource officers may encounter a higher proportion of minor in possession of alcohol or drug violations. Officers assigned to enforce motor carrier laws may report filing a high proportion of overweight violations.

– What an officer is asked to do determines what types of violations he will look for. Police departments routinely evaluate traffic accidents and patterns. When a common reason for an increase in traffic accidents (e.g., speeding, following too closely) is identified it is legitimate, and even expected, that a department will encourage its officers to focus their enforcement time on that behavior.

– Agency funding often influences the types of violations that are enforced. During the days of the federally mandated 55 miles per hour speed limit on the interstate highway system, state patrols were often asked to provide evidence that they were aggressively enforcing speed violations. Such proof was necessary to avoid the loss of federal highway funds. Some agencies conducted periodic covert speed surveys. Others demonstrated that their officers were writing an increasing number of speeding tickets. For many officers this meant increasing their stops for speed violations so as to avoid being the least productive. More recently, when departments receive grants to encourage seat belt use, their officers are encouraged (lured by the promise of overtime pay) to aggressively enforce seat belt violations.

– An officer's personal experience may influence the kinds of violations he considers important enough to initiate a traffic stop. An officer who is a new parent or who recently worked a fatality accident involving children may be encouraged by this experience to enforce the seat belt law. And of course, there are some driving behaviors that really tick some officers off enough (e.g., road rage) to enforce them vigorously.

There is really nothing wrong with an officer developing a personal preference toward one type of violation or another. For example, in a recent racial profiling case an officer was questioned about the validity of the charge that caused him to initiate the traffic stop. The truck driver was stopped because the mud flaps on his trailer were too short. The plaintiff's attorney attempted to suggest that this was a bogus violation and was only used as a pretext to stop his client. The officer explained that mud flaps are an important safety issue and then demonstrated that he had in fact stopped many other drivers for mud flap violations. Undaunted, the plaintiff's attorney questioned why this officer wrote so many tickets for this violation when few other officers statewide do so. The officer produced information demonstrating that motor vehicle accidents had been caused in his area by debris and rainwater thrown onto other cars by short or non-existent mud flaps. In effect, the officer demonstrated that his focus on mud flap violations was based on a legitimate public safety concern in his area.

In contrast, consider the following case. During a motion to suppress hearing, a police officer was being questioned about the violation that caused him to initiate the stop. The violation was an obstructed inside rearview mirror, which is against the law in that particular state. The attorney asked the officer how many times he had stopped somebody for this violation, to which the officer replied, "Dozens of times." A review of this officer's stopping performance confirmed that he had in fact stopped nearly 50 motorists for this violation in the previous year. Incidentally, in this case the "obstruction" was a small green string draped around and in front of the inside rearview mirror upon which a paper air freshener in the shape of a pine tree dangled. A further evaluation of this officer's stop records revealed that in nearly every case wherein he reported this violation the person stopped was African-American. About a third of these stops occurred at night and nearly half occurred on an interstate highway. Less than ten percent of these stops resulted in the issuance of a citation and nearly 90 percent involved a consent search. Furthermore, he was the only officer in his department that reported making stops for this obscure traffic violation and there was no evidence that this driving behavior was a direct or indirect cause of traffic accidents. Ultimately, the court ruled in favor of the plaintiff, ruled the evidence obtained in the search inadmissible and dismissed the drug possession case.

Avoiding the "Popularity" Trap

The lessons here are rather straightforward.

The following guidelines are recommended to avoid the popularity trap, or worse, the perception that patrol officers are using the traffic code as a mere pretext for conducting more invasive searches.

–*Have a legitimate reason for each stop and don't be reluctant to articulate this to the violator.* The term "legitimate" is used in this context to mean violations that can be attributed as the cause of serious threats to public safety.

–*Document the effect that enforcement needs have on the reasons why officers make stops.* Even an increase in the use of minor violations can be legitimate if these behaviors are related to a current enforcement demand. For example, an increase in stops relating to vehicle registration violations may be justified when voluntary compliance decreases. Similarly, one should expect to see an increase in stops relating to seat belt violations among the officers assigned to a task force that is deployed to 'encourage' seat belt use.

–*Avoid an over reliance on minor, favorite or pet peeve violations.* An analysis of stop rationales at the individual level may reveal inconsistent patterns among officers. At some level this is normal and reflects the officers' individual preferences. However, the overuse of minor violations by an individual officer may be considered questionable.

–*Avoid offender profiles that specify or suggest race and ethnicity.* Research consistently finds that race and ethnicity are very poor indicators of criminal propensity. There is simply no evidence that individuals of a particular race or ethnicity are more likely to be engaged in criminal behaviors. Other factors that might suggest race (e.g., listening to rap music, wearing gaudy jewelry, etc.) are equally ineffective indicators of criminal behavior.

–*Focus on what is there, not what might be there.* While the value of an experienced police officer's "hunch" is well documented, the focus of a traffic stop should begin and end with the driver's behavior that motivated the officer to initiate the stop. Secondary considerations (e.g., the desire to search, drug interdiction procedures) are just that – secondary. These considerations should occur subsequent to a resolution of the primary alleged violation that initiated the stop.

Analyzing Why Motorists Are Stopped

In the early years of the racial profiling controversy a police chief was asked by a reporter, "Why do police officers stop some cars and not others?" The police chief quipped a response, "Because some people break the law and others don't!" Good answer, but, that is really not what the reporter wanted to know. It is a given that most drivers will at one time or another violate the traffic law and in doing so place themselves at risk of being stopped. Some of us violate traffic laws more frequently than others, but eventually we all fail to signal a lane change, drive a bit too fast, or forget to check the light over our license plate.

Experienced police officers are well aware that most drivers, when observed long enough, will eventually commit a traffic violation sufficient to establish probable cause for a stop. Once the motorist is stopped, the officer may issue a verbal warning, a written warning, a citation and may even arrest the motorist. During the stop a police officer may request a consent search, gather probable cause for a search warrant, or request assistance from a K-9 officer. All of this occurs in the absence of active supervision.

Because of their ubiquitous nature, discretionary character and ability to perform as the primary gateway into the criminal justice system for most criminal defendants, the police stop has become a major issue in the racial profiling controversy. It is logical therefore for us to ask the question, "Why do the police stop some cars and not others?"

Why Worry About This?

The most viable and far-reaching legal remedy for a person alleging racial profiling is likely the pattern and practice statute (Title 42, U.S.C., Section 14141). This law was passed as part of the Crime Control Act of 1994. The statute makes it unlawful:

[F]or any governmental authority, or agent thereof, or any person acting on behalf of a government authority, to engage in a pattern or practice of conduct by law enforcement officers or by officials or employees of any governmental agency ... that deprives persons of rights, privileges, or immunities secured or protected by the constitution or laws of the United States.

Only the United States Attorney General has the authority to file a case under this section. The law is designed to address patterns and practices of abuse. This statute has been effective in various cases involving excessive force, harassment, false arrest, coercive sexual conduct and unlawful searches and seizures. This provision was used quite effectively in the case that led to the acceptance of a consent decree by the New Jersey State Police during the Clinton Administration. These cases focus on the entire pattern and practice of a department's enforcement program. There is no need for an individual defendant. Although the law does not provide for punitive damages, losing such a challenge can have a profound effect on a department's routine operations.

For all practical purposes, the U.S. Department of Justice ignored this statute during the Bush Administration. There is increasing evidence that the current Obama Administration is interested in pursuing racial profiling litigations based on this provision. Ultimately these cases will be decided on the statistical evaluation of a department's pattern and practices relating to traffic stops and the persons involved.

Of course, should this prediction come true then it is likely that the pattern analysis will be broader than a mere evaluation of the reasons why motorists are stopped. A more comprehensive discussion of analytical techniques for racial profiling studies is the subject of a previous chapter. For now, the focus is on evaluating the reasons behind why motorists are stopped to identify a potential disparity.

Important Data Limitations
The variables in a police stop data set are seldom evaluated separately. While most analysts will include frequency tables illustrating the distribution of individual variables, the most insightful analyses involve the combinations of variables. For example, the analyst may present a table illus-

trating the most frequent reasons police officers use to initiate traffic stops. The following Table 12 is an example.

Table 12 – *General reason for stop.*

Reported reason	Frequency	Percentage
Moving violation	19,870	53.1
DUI/DL Check Lane	88	.2
Probable cause	582	1.6
Suspicious circumstances	1,733	4.6
Defective equipment	4,252	11.4
Service rendered	1,032	2.8
Pedestrian stop	666	1.8
Traffic accident	7,299	19.5
Miscellaneous	1,811	4.8
Not reported	121	.3
Total	37,454	100.1

NOTE: Percentages may exceed 100.0% due to rounding error.

Because the reported reasons for the stops are so broadly measured, these tables will not produce particularly important findings. In Table 12, "Moving violation" constitutes the majority of the reasons why individuals were stopped by this department. Within this category there is considerable variation with respect to the seriousness of this charge. A moving violation could be as serious as ten miles per hour over the limit in an occupied school zone or as benign as five miles over the limit on a sparsely traveled section of an interstate highway. This data limitation is a common problem in racial profiling research and creates important analytical challenges.

What Should Happen

Often the best way to begin analyzing anything is to make some assumptions on what you expect to find.

When evaluating the reasons behind why police officers make stops there are some routine expectations.

- In most departments, speeding violations are the most common reason for a stop.
- Patterns (in the reasons for the stops) are generally considered legitimate if they are consistent with the officer's assignment.
- Patterns (in the reasons for the stops) are generally considered legitimate when there is consistency among all officers and particularly among similarly situated officers.

What Should Not Happen

These limitations notwithstanding, there are a few research findings that cause concerns between racial profiling researchers and problems for police departments defending themselves against a racial profiling accusation. For example:

–An unexplained change in the reasons that officers report as the motivation for initiating traffic stops from one year to the next. Slight variations in the percentages of stops by reason are common and not particularly notable from one reporting period to the next. In very large departments or for data sets that span a long time a notable change in the percentage of stops for any single reason would require a considerable change in the actual number of stops for that reason. Because this variable is broadly measured, an increase or decrease in the percentage of stops predicated on a single statute may not be identifiable. For example, if a department receives a grant to pay officers overtime for seat belt enforcement then an increase in stops for this reason would not be measured if this charge were considered one (of many) type of moving violation. The key evaluative issue here is an "unexplained change." Policing resources (in the form of officers on the street available to make stops) are relatively stable. A substantial percentage increase in one type of stop always results in a percentage decrease in other types of stops. Therefore, the most important question to ask in this type of analysis is whether a substantial change in the reasons for stops from one reporting period to another can be attributed to a legitimate or intended change of policing strategy.

–A substantial difference between an individual officer and his similarly situated peers relating to the reported reasons for stops. Officers who are similarly situated (e.g., working the same beats at the same time) tend to do the same things. After all, in most cases similarly situated officers are exposed to the same populations of drivers, traffic patterns and enforcement demands. As a result, one would expect that a pattern will emerge with respect to what these officers report as the reasons for the stops they make. Of course some variation is inevitable. The most important issue here is whether a particular officer is doing something very different from what his similarly situated peers are doing. For example, let's assume that during the course of a year the ten officers assigned to a particular beat and shift report a total of 20 stops for an inoperable license plate light. This alone would not be a particularly alarming finding unless 18 of the stops were initiated by one of these ten officers. In many cases, however, it is not possible to identify a group of similarly situated officers. This is especially true in departments with large jurisdictions, such as state police agencies, or for officers who are assigned to narrowly focused enforcement strategies, such as gang units.

–A substantial percentage of overall stops for reasons that are not directly related to legitimate public safety concerns. The reasons motorists are stopped exhibit a rather consistent pattern. The majority of all stops involve moving violations and most of these are related to speeding. This pattern is consistent throughout the nation. Beyond this it is important to look for a large number of stops based on reasons that are unrelated to actual public safety concerns. Excessive stops for dirty license plates, inoperable lights (during daylight hours), "suspicion," "investigative," or for "miscellaneous" reasons appear to be questionable. These types of stops are particularly problematic when they appear to involve drivers from one particular racial or ethnic group. For example, if an officer reports a large percentage of his vehicle stops are predicated on the charge of "excessive noise" and the analysis of these stops reveals that the large majority of them involve young African-American drivers who are playing their radios too loud then one might question the public safety need of these stops.

–A discrepancy between the relative severity of the driver's behavior prior to the stop and the punitiveness of the officer's enforcement decision. It is reasonable to expect that an individual stopped for a serious violation is more likely to receive a citation. Alternatively, an individual stopped for a relatively minor violation would more likely receive a warning. There should be some relationship between the severity of the driver's behavior (in terms of its threat to public safety) and the level of "punishment" administered by the officer initiating the stop. Of course there will be exceptions. Sometimes individuals are stopped for serious violations and then after the initial face to face contact the officer decides that the most appropriate response would be a verbal warning. For example, a speeder on the way to visit a dying relative may be merely given a verbal admonition to drive safer. The opposite may also be true. An individual stopped for failing to signal a lane change on a sparsely traveled roadway may be found to be driving under the influence of alcohol. Most police stop data sets, however, do not measure this information adequately to perform these types of analyses. This type of analysis requires ordinal, internal or ratio level data, that is, variable attributes that can be arranged in some logical fashion. The variable attributes that describe the officer's enforcement decision (i.e., arrest, citation, written warning, verbal warning, no action) can be arranged in terms of their level of punitiveness. Arrests are more punitive than citations. Citations are more punitive than written warnings, and so forth. The reason for the stop are typically measured nominally and very broadly. The attributes of this variable usually include moving violation, equipment violation, traffic accident, etc. These attributes cannot be arranged in terms of their level of seriousness. There are very serious and very minor violations in each of these categories. Some equipment violations are more serious than some moving violations, and vice versa. As a result in most cases it is not possible to correlate (i.e., find a relationship) between the seriousness of the driver's behavior prior to the stop and the punitiveness of the officer's enforcement decision. The only solution to this problem would be to add a variable to the police stop data that describes the relative seriousness (on a scale from 1 – 10) of the driver's behavior that caused the officer to initiate the stop.

–A difference in the types of, reasons for or severity of stops between racial and ethnic groups. One of the most serious accusations within the racial profiling controversy is that the police stop racial and ethnic minorities for less serious violations. Early on in the controversy quite a few researchers predicted that because racial and ethnic minorities tended to be more economically disadvantaged then these drivers would be more likely to be stopped for equipment violations. Their logic was simple. Poorer people are less able to maintain their vehicles and therefore more susceptible to being stopped for an equipment violation. In the hundreds of racial profiling studies done so far, there is no evidence of this. In fact, study after study reports no differences in the type of, reasons for or severity of stops between racial and ethnic groups. Such a finding might, if true, support the notion that the police are more likely to initiate pretextual stops involving racial and ethnic drivers. Given the lack of detail in how this variable (i.e., reason for the stop) is measured, it is not likely a researcher would be able to conduct such an analysis. Besides, there are so many other contextual factors beyond the driver's behavior that legitimately influence a police officer's decision to stop that are never captured in police stop data sets. Therefore, it is not likely such an analysis would be able to identify real differences in the reasons for stops between drivers of different racial or ethnic groups.

–An over-representation of drivers (within one racial or ethnic group) who are stopped for relatively minor violations, subjected to (or asked) a consent search, not issued a citation and not found in possession of contraband. In routine police operations events are interconnected. Few things happen by themselves. Criminal justice is a process whereby one decision is influenced by the decisions that precede it and then influences the decisions that follow. Racial profiling researchers, and especially litigators, attempt to connect stop events in order to produce a pattern of behavior. These analyses produce findings like, "Hispanic drivers are stopped for less serious violations and when stopped are more likely to be searched, less likely to be found in possession of contraband, and less likely to be issued a citation." In most cases it is not possible to measure the actual seriousness of the driver's behavior prior to the stop, much less between

racial and ethnic groups. Most police stop data sets do not contain information on an officer's motivation (e.g., presence of sensory evidence of a violation like the smell of marijuana, contradictions in the information obtained from drivers and passengers, documentation inconsistencies, etc.) for conducting a consent search. In the absence of this it is not possible for an analyst to measure the relative influence of a driver's race on the probability of a consent search. The legality of a search is not determined by what it produces or fails to produce. The legality of a stop is determined by whether or not its process is consistent with Constitutional guidelines. Finally, the decision to issue a citation is influenced by dozens of factors in addition to the severity of the driver's behavior. Most of this information is not collected within the stop data set. Finally, in responding to this finding it is important to remember that aggregate patterns do not account for the contextual factors that influence police decision making at the individual level. There is no such thing as a "routine traffic stop." Every stop includes numerous factors that all play a role in a police officer's decision making. Unless and until these factors are adequately identified and measured then it is irresponsible to assume the differences among them can be attributed primarily to the race or ethnicity of the driver.

7

Why Officers Should Stick to the Script and Close the Deal

Many years ago my sergeant wrote on my annual performance evaluation, "Trooper Withrow should refrain from embellishing the approved Seven Step Violator Contact." I had developed the habit of engaging in idle chit-chat with violators. I thought this was good for public relations. The idea that a police officer should follow a proscribed script during a citizen contact seemed to me at the time a bit restraining. I was wrong. The seven step violator contact and other similar scripts are important for maintaining enforcement consistency, officer safety, and validating police officer professionalism. Such scripts are becoming important in the racial profiling controversy.

Enhancing the Perceived Legitimacy of the Stop

How many times have we read a newspaper story wherein an alleged victim of racial profiling says, "I was stopped for no good reason," and later learned that they in fact paid a fine for a bona fide, or even serious, traffic violation? The alleged victim's statement seems inconsistent with his behavior. If the alleged victim was stopped for a bogus violation then why did he pay the fine? What the alleged victim probably means is, "I do not consider the stop to be for a legitimate reason, because I do this all the time and never get stopped, other people do this and don't get stopped, or the officer was just looking for a reason to stop me because I am (fill in the blank)."

Questions about the legitimacy or appropriateness of a traffic stop do not reside wholly within the minority community. Indeed, there are numerous examples of non-minority drivers who question an officer's motivation. For example, have you ever heard a person ask, "Why are you stopping me when you should be out looking for *real* criminals?" Or,

"Where were you last week when I got cut off in traffic by a speeder?" Often the police try to defend themselves by pointing out that traffic violations are in fact crimes that do threaten public and individual safety more frequently than real crime. But these responses don't seem to satisfy the accusers. At some level these criticisms are merely defense mechanisms delivered by violators who have a psychological need to blame somebody else for their discretions. Beyond this, the research suggests that there are six common factors that tend to enhance the perceived legitimacy of a traffic stop or police/citizen contact.

Make a Preliminary Enforcement Decision Prior to the Stop

Some driving behaviors (e.g., speeding in a school zone, passing on a hill) are almost universally considered "ticketable." Few officers would issue warnings in such situations. Other offenses (e.g., an inoperable tail light) usually result in a warning. As a general rule, a police officer should make a preliminary enforcement decision (i.e., citation, warning, etc.) prior to making face to face contact with a violator. In doing so, officers will be more consistent in their enforcement decision making. Furthermore, the officer's enforcement decisions will likely be more influenced by actual driving behavior, rather than the violator's attitude. Of course, during some stops information becomes available that may warrant a change in the officer's preliminary enforcement decision. When this occurs then the officer has every right to amend his preliminary decision. Most stops, however, do not include extenuating circumstances and those that do are generally easily recalled by the officer when asked to explain why an alternative decision was made. The objective of this recommendation is to ensure some objective relationship exists between a driver's behavior and a police officer's enforcement decision.

Justify the Decision to Stop

Some drivers consider traffic violations to be relatively minor offenses and not worth a police officer's time. Relatively speaking, they are correct. Traffic violations are a minor inconvenience and result in small fines while criminal offenses can result in big fines and even jail/prison time. This does not, however, mean that traffic violations are unimportant. Deaths, personal injuries and property damage caused by traffic violations are considerably higher and more common than those caused by violent crimes. Vigorous traffic enforcement is a legitimate public safety strategy and an effective criminal interdiction tool. These are appropriate responses when a police officer is asked by a driver to justify the appropriateness of a traffic stop. In most cases, drivers understand these justifications and while not pleased about being stopped they at least understand the relative importance of the enforcement strategy. The few drivers who are unimpressed by this explanation are really not upset that the police vigorously enforce the traffic law. They are just upset that THEY were stopped. Frankly, there is not much a police officer can do when the driver has personalized the contact.

Stop for Real Reasons

In most states there are thousands of reasons a person can be legally stopped. For the most part, each of these statutes responds to a legitimate public safety concern. One exception might be in Oklahoma where it is illegal to read a comic book while driving. Recently a Dallas police officer wrote a lady a ticket for "failure to speak English," which would have been a valid violation had the lady been a commercial truck driver. There should be some connection between the reasons for the stops and legitimate threats to public safety. Numerous stops for dirty license plates make little sense during daylight hours. In addition, the overuse of certain relatively minor violations is often interpreted as abusive and may suggest the use of pretextual stops.

Separate the Stop from the Search

At the very heart of the racial profiling controversy is the perception that racial and ethnic minorities are stopped for relatively minor violations because the police really want to conduct a search. Critics of the police argue that the stated reasons for such stops are merely pretexts and that the police officers' real motivation is based on a belief that racial and ethnic minorities are more likely to possess contraband. Alleged victims of racial profiling consistently point out that they get stopped and searched frequently yet seldom ticketed.

This produces a perception that the police are really more interested in hassling minority drivers than they are in enforcing the traffic law. The solution to this is to separate the stop event from the search event. Often the best way to do this is to complete the stop transaction (preferably resulting in the issuance of a valid citation) and then, if justified, initiate the search event. As a general rule, a police officer should never begin a traffic stop with a request to conduct a consent search. Furthermore, every traffic stop that involves a search should also include documentation (in the form of a warning or citation) of the initial reason for the stop.

Sticking to the Script

The *Seven Step Violator Contact* is so old and well-entrenched in American policing that nobody really knows where it came from. Versions of this procedure have been taught in police academies for decades. Few procedures are as enduring.

The Seven Step Violator Contact

1. Greeting and identification of agency and officer
2. Statement of violation committed
3. Identification of driver and check conditions of violator and vehicle
4. Statement of action to be taken
5. Take that action
6. Explain what the violator must do
7. Leave

When a police officer follows a proscribed script, extraneous information (usually in the form of argumentative statements from the violator) is less likely to become a part of the contact. This does not mean that an officer should not be responsive to a legitimate comment from a violator or ignore factors that threaten his personal safety. Police officers should be encouraged to offer explanations and look for personal threats. But in doing so some officers tend to get distracted and allow the contact to deviate from its purpose. In a way, following a script is like using a daily task list. When a person becomes distracted, and we all inevitably do, having a list available that contains the tasks we are supposed to be working on that day helps us maintain focus on the important things. A standard contact procedure provides this level of direction and allows an officer, momentarily distracted by irrelevant information or comments, the ability to get back on message.

The seven steps are interdependent in that no single step is more important than another. When used together they tend to objectify violator contacts and keep officers on task. Within the broad context of police/community relations and the more narrow issue of racial profiling, the seventh step appears to be particularly critical. A substantial portion of citizen complaints emerge from interactions between police officers and citizens occurring after the contact has, or should have been, terminated. Although no empirical research has been done on this it appears that many citizen complaints could be avoided had the police officer simply turned around and left once the contact is completed rather than responded to an incendiary comment from a violator.

Closing the Deal

The absence of a citation during an alleged racial profiling incident is a recurring theme in racial profiling "stories." Often police officers merely ignore the initial reason for the stop once the violator is found to be in possession of contraband or when evidence of a more serious crime is revealed. This is a mistake. It is very difficult for an alleged racial profiling victim to argue that he was not legally stopped when he was issued a citation or warning, and better yet paid a fine. As a general rule, police officers should be guided by the notion that if the driver's behavior is serious enough to justify the stop (and their time) then it is serious enough to justify writing a ticket or warning.

8

Your Message Matters

During the mid-1990s, the State of New Jersey was ground zero in the racial profiling controversy. A group of racial and ethnic minorities accused the New Jersey State Police of racial profiling. The first major racial profiling study was conducted at the request of the judge hearing this case. Ultimately the State of New Jersey was forced to accept an immensely controlling consent decree that only recently has expired. In the midst of this emerging controversy, New Jersey State Police Colonel Carl Williams publically stated, "Two weeks ago the President of the United States went to Mexico to talk to the President of Mexico about drugs. He didn't go to Ireland. He didn't go to England." Colonel Williams was attempting to justify his troopers' tendency to focus their drug interdiction efforts on Mexicans or Hispanics, ostensibly because most illegal drugs come from Central and South America. One assumes that if most illegal drugs came from Ireland or England then he would encourage his troopers to stop Irish and English drivers. Governor Christie Whitman fired Colonel Williams the next day.

When responding to the racial profiling controversy, the leader's message matters a great deal. What the chief or sheriff says in response to the controversy is internalized, and often personalized, by the officers and deputies. Even more importantly, what the leader does communicates important messages. In short, the leader's message and behavior matters because they have profound effects on organizational behavior.

Within the context of the racial profiling controversy, the effectiveness of a leader's message depends on the context within which it is delivered. There are two important contexts. *Proactive* messages occur prior to accusations of racial profiling. *Reactive* messages occur after a department has been accused of racial profiling.

Proactive Messages

These types of messages occur prior to a department being accused of racial profiling. They should be designed to ensure that police officers are aware of the racial profiling controversy and to communicate that the department is attempting to prevent racial profiling. Regardless of its content, the leader's message should be comprehensive and consistent.

Comprehensiveness

Comprehensive means that all possible situations in which racial profiling behaviors could occur are considered and controlled.

The leader's comprehensive message should include:

- A clearly written policy that both defines and prohibits behaviors that might be considered racial profiling.

- An ongoing program for collecting and analyzing police stops.

- An effective training program designed to make officers aware of how their behaviors might be considered racial profiling.

- A general enforcement policy that:
  - Describes behaviors that warrant a traffic stop,
  - Appropriately controls consent searches, and
  - Encourages officers to follow a specific contact process.

- Deployment strategies that rely on demand indicators (e.g., citizen calls for service, reported crime) that are produced separate from department activities.

- How technology (if available) should be used to document traffic stops.

- An active strategy for hiring and retaining a racially/ethically reflective work force.

- A revision to those portions the department's incentive structure (if any) that reward officers more for drug and asset seizures.

Consistency

Consistency means that the message is the same through-out the department. All policies, procedures and programs supported by the department must be governed by a principal that does not tolerate racial profiling behavior. This includes how a leader responds to officers found guilty of racial profiling as well as the leader's response to overtly racist remarks. If a patrol officer violates the department's racial profiling policy when he stops a suspect because of the suspect's race then so would a detective if he makes an arrest based on the same thing. Openly racist remarks, jokes, cartoons and other expressions should be swiftly and publically chastised. Even seemingly innocent remarks should be questioned. For example, if an officer refers to his assigned beat as "The Hood" because the residents of the beat are predominantly African-American or "Little Mexico" because the residents of the beat are predominantly Hispanic, then the leader's response should be unequivocal. No such remarks are allowable because they engender an image of a neigh-borhood or its residents that may be construed to be evidence of racist attitudes.

Reactive Messages

These types of messages occur after a department is accused of racial profiling. They should be designed to communicate that the department is aware of a potential problem and is actively seeking information to determine the veracity of the accusation.

Responding to a Racial Profiling Study

When responding to a racial profiling study, it is important to remember that such studies seldom produce definitive proof of racial profiling, at least objectively. The best they can do is demonstrate that racial and ethnic minorities *might* be over-represented in stops. This of course assumes that the benchmark estimating the racial and ethnic proportions within the driving population is accurate (and they seldom are) and that all other factors (i.e., differential deployment patterns) have been considered (and they seldom are).

Criticisms of the study often fall on deaf ears. At the individual level, perceptions of the police department are relatively static. Racial profiling studies seldom change people's attitudes about the police. Citizens who consistently support the police are not usually convinced that the officers engage in racial profiling and some of these citizens might even mistakenly consider such practices essential to good policing. Critics of the police may feel vindicated if the research is consistent with their previously developed opinions of the police. Therefore, direct criticisms of a racial profiling study's results are rather futile.

Instead the leader's attention should be on developing policies and procedures designed to address the issues revealed by the research. At the very least the department should consider adopting a policy that defines and prohibits racial profiling. Secondarily, because most racial profiling studies reveal inefficient enforcement patterns, changes to policies and procedures are often warranted.

This does not, however, mean that the department should merely accept the study's findings. Some racial profiling studies are seriously flawed. These methodological flaws should be discussed openly, but not be relied upon as an excuse to completely discount the study's results. Just because a researcher makes a mistake does not necessarily mean that his entire effort is useless. Although racial profiling studies seldom provide definitive proof of racial profiling, they are quite useful to administrators because they often contain important insights into how police officers work. In fact, prior to the racial profiling controversy, we knew very little about the dynamics of traffic stops. Racial profiling data does produce some useful information and the leader should communicate his willingness to use this information to the extent he can.

Responding to a Racial Profiling Accusation
When responding to a specific racial profiling accusation it is important for the leader to be extremely cautious. Accusations of racial profiling are quite similar to any other type of police misconduct allegation.

Regardless of whether the allegation involves a single officer/incident or the department as a whole, the response should occur in the following steps.

–Acknowledge receipt and understanding of the complaint. At this point the leader should avoid at all cost making any judgments regarding the veracity of the complaint. This is not the time to discuss the complaint's merits or lack thereof. Often the most effective way to do this is to merely or, better yet, proactively acknowledge that a complaint has been received.

–Assure the public that a thorough investigation will be conducted. At this point there is very little that the leader can or should communicate. The investigation process is likely already established by law or policy. It is usually a good idea to remind the public of how such investigations are handled. It is, however, never a good idea to agree to a departure from your current procedures or to a time line. Internal investigations policies are there for a reason, and it is essential for everybody involved that these be followed.

–Conduct the appropriate investigation. At this point the investigation should adhere to its usual process. It is critically important for the leader not to intervene in this process until it is (according to policy) appropriate for him to do so.

–Respond to public inquiries when appropriate. At some point the investigation or inquiry will be completed. While adhering to the various statutes and/or labor agreements regarding the public disclosure of information relating to internal investigations and police officers, the leader should communicate as much as possible to the public. To most people the details and results of the investigation are not nearly as important as the fact that a thorough investigation was conducted.

The Special Case of the "S-Word"

Racial profiling issues are often emotionally charged. In fact, the mere utterance of the accusation within the context of a routine police stop is often enough to elevate what would have been a routine citizen complaint into something more serious, and more public. As a general rule, police administrators should be responsive to citizens who lodge complaints. It is important that the public be confident that if an officer misbehaves the police department will do something about it. It is equally important for the police administrator to ensure that the officer accused of misbehavior be afforded all the procedural rights available to him.

There are times, however, when a police administrator is justified in ending a conversation with a complaining citizen. That time occurs when the citizen utters the S-word, which is "sue." Anytime an individual seriously communicates their desire or threat to initiate a lawsuit then a police administrator is justified in referring the citizen to his legal counsel and abruptly ending the conversation. Lawsuits are serious matters, and if a citizen is motivated to initiate litigation then continuing the conversation is futile and may even exacerbate the problem.

Getting Help

The issues surrounding the racial profiling controversy and the research that arises from it are complicated and multi-dimensional. More importantly, stakeholders and more than a few spectators, are quite willing to hold forth with a statement which they believe accurately represents the manner in which police officers make decisions and perform their daily tasks. While most of these individuals and groups are well intentioned, they are often misinformed. In the words of the great American humorist Mark Twain, "It ain't what you know that gets you into trouble. It's what you know for sure that just ain't so."

Because the racial profiling controversy is so contentious and emerging (new things are being learned every day), it is important to have a partner in the journey. More than a few police leaders have opted to hire outside assistance when confronted with a racial profiling problem—and for good reason. External assistance is often viewed as more objective and less beholden to (i.e., influenced by) the organizational demands of the police organization. A few years ago I was asked to conduct a racial profiling study for a large Midwestern police department. After the data was in—but before the analyses were complete—the police chief asked me, "What should I do if the data show minorities are over-represented?"

This question was asked at a time when nearly every study in every department revealed that some minority drivers are over-represented in stops. In this environment, an alternative finding would have been remarkable. I responded, "Chief I am more worried about how people will respond if I find out there is no over-representation." Ultimately, the study revealed that African-American drivers are over-represented in stops. This "validated" the feelings expressed by certain members of the community and the most vocal groups. The data were, however, not convincing enough to conclude racial profiling. The point is the study was done by someone independent of the police department. Furthermore, the data were given to the local media and the results of their analysis came to the same conclusions. In other words, the department avoided the need to justify the objectivity of the study, because they actually did not analyze the data.

So, what type of person should you look for? There are more than a few academic types and consultants who are more than willing to accept the taxpayers' money. But are they qualified?

An effective research partner for a racial profiling study should:

– *Have a thorough understanding of routine police systems and procedures.* Your research partner should intimately know the nuances of routine police operations. This includes a detailed knowledge of the factors that influence officer decision making. For example, your research partner should not be surprised to learn that the contextual features of a stop event (e.g., time of day, location, number of officers involved, etc.) influence the outcome of a stop event in meaningful ways.

– *Understand the limitations of the stop data.* Police stop data do not contain enough information to make definitive conclusions about an officer's motivation. For example, the data do not accurately record whether the officer actually knew the race or ethnicity of the driver before the stop. As a result, it is rather difficult to allege that the driver's race or ethnicity was the factor that influenced the officer's decision to stop if we cannot prove that the officer knew this information prior to the decision to stop. Also, the order of stop events often cannot be established. For example, a small percentage of stops involve a police/citizen confrontation and an arrest. The stop data often cannot determine which of these events occurred first.

– *Understand the legalities associated with police stops and criminal procedures.* Police officers are constrained by law and department procedure. These constraints affect police decision making in significant ways. For example, police officers in most jurisdictions are required to conduct an inventory search when they seize a motor vehicle. The purpose of these searches is to protect the department from liability. Because they are required by policy, the police officer has no choice but to initiate the search. As a result, these searches are non-discretionary and should be considered separately in a racial profiling study.

– *Understand the differences between seemingly similar stop events.* Stop events appear to the uninformed to be similar. They are not. The most important distinction is discretion. Police/citizen contacts predicated by a citizen call for service are nondiscretionary while routine traffic stops are highly discretionary. Searches also vary with respect to their level of discretion. Searches incident to an arrest and inventory searches are nondiscretionary, while consent searches are highly discretionary. Arrests also are based on different justifications. When a police officer encounters evidence of a crime he generally has the authority to initiate an arrest, or not. On the other hand, if during the stop the officer learns of the existence of an active arrest warrant for that driver then the officer has no choice but to initiate the arrests. The ability to differentiate between seemingly similar stop events, with respect to the level of discretion available to the officer, is a critical skill for a racial profiling analyst.

– *Have a strong background in research methods.* The ability to develop solid variables that have enough attributes to produce a comprehensive understanding of how the police make stops and deal with drivers is an essential skill. Research methods are not easy. Collecting data is a difficult chore, particularly within the context of social science when it is often not possible to identify all the possible outcomes.

Your research partner should be able to demonstrate his methodological skills, in the form of published articles, books and reports that were conducted in similar contexts.

   – Be able to conduct and interpret routine statistical information within the context of where the data are collected. Even the most complicated statistical models can be developed with a minimum level of training. Conversely, even the simplest statistics can be misunderstood if the analyst has no understanding of the context in which the data arise. Numbers are easy. Understanding what numbers mean is hard. For example, a recent racial profiling study revealed that an officer, we will call him Smith, tended to stop a substantially higher percentage of Hispanic drivers than his similarly assigned peers. Initially, there was some concern that Officer Smith might be discriminating against Hispanic drivers. The researcher later found that Officer Smith (despite his Anglo-Saxon surname) was often the only officer assigned to the night shift who spoke Spanish. The non-Spanish-speaking officers routinely asked Officer Smith to handle these cases and Officer Smith correctly reported them as his own case. So, while it appeared that Officer Smith was racial profiling, he actually was not. Incidentally, Officer Smith's mother is from Spain and he is married to a Hispanic woman. Oftentimes it is important to look behind the data for the answer.

Diversity *(In All Its Forms)* Makes You Stronger

When most people hear the word "diversity" they think in terms of race, ethnicity or gender. Organizations are encouraged, and in some cases required, to maintain certain levels of diversity, with respect to the race, ethnicity and gender of their employees. True diversity is, however, more diverse than that. There is diversity in culture, religion, politics, socioeconomic status, physical ability, mental capacity, attitude, experience, education and so on. Diversity cannot necessarily be achieved by merely hiring individuals of different races, ethnicities or genders. Just because an employee is a racial minority does not mean that he or she will either represent or advocate the "minority experience."

The objective of diversity is ultimately to ensure all perspectives of an issue are considered and that organizations will behave in ways that are sensitive to the various and often conflicting demands of the public they serve. Theoretically, diverse organizations, at least to the extent they are representative of the populations they serve, are more capable of optimizing decisions so that all affected individuals and groups are equitably served. The purpose of this chapter is to discuss how paying attention to diversity, in all its forms, can enable a police department to respond ethically to the racial profiling controversy.

Why Diversity Matters More in Policing

The police are often characterized as a "visible" public service. Despite the fact that other public services are used more frequently (e.g., water, sewer, trash, roads, etc.) the police are the most visible reminder of the power of government. The visibility of the police department within the context of other public services is rather perplexing. Citizens use other public services far more frequently. We appreciate the municipal water and wastewater department every time we take a bath, flush a toilet or drink a glass of water, but we never think about the employees who work at the plant. The trash and recycling trucks come to most homes weekly, far more frequently than the police department, but we would not likely recognize our local 'sanitation engineers' unless they were riding on the back of the truck. On a daily basis we appreciate the availability of paved streets and traffic control devices that enable us to get to work and back home safely, but we don't care who takes care of these amenities as long as the potholes are filled.

So why is the police department so "visible" and why is diversity more important?

First, unlike other city service providers, the police by virtue of their arrest authority can threaten our individual liberty. Since the beginning of our republic, Americans have had a healthy distrust of unchecked power and autonomous public agencies. There is a reason why we do not have a national police force, the police are routinely required to seek approval from an independent magistrate, and the police are responsible to civilian (i.e., political) authority. We tend to hold the police to a higher behavioral standard because our Founding Fathers distrusted tyrannical power. We are more confident that the police will be accountable to us when we perceive that the police department is representative of us.

Second, many decisions made by police departments and individual police officers are subjective, and therefore controversial. When the water does not work, the trash is not picked up or a pothole remains unfilled we know exactly what we want those responsible to do – fix the water line, pick up the trash and fill the pothole. These are objective performance standards. The only controversy is when they are left undone. Once these deficiencies are tended to we move on and soon forget about them. Not so with the police. There are few objective and universally acceptable performance standards in policing. We want the police to enforce the law, that is, until we get stopped and issued a ticket. We want the police to regularly patrol our neighborhood, but not to the point where we feel threatened by their presence. We want the police to be visible until a patrol car parked on the side of the road snarls traffic. For the most part, however, we accept police decisions even though they affect us adversely when we perceive that the police have been fair. The perception of fairness in police decision making depends largely on whether or not the decision makers considered all perspectives during the decision-making process. We don't like to be ignored. We want our voices heard. We want to share our perspective. Public organizations that are capable of considering diverse perspectives are considered "fairer." Even the most ardent critics of the police are more likely to accept an adverse decision when they believe their interests have been considered. Highly diverse organizations and the people that work in them, that value multiple perspectives while making decisions, are in a better position to ensure voluntary compliance.

Finally, public image is important, particularly for taxpayer-supported organizations like the police. Police agencies that allow their public image to degrade will often find it difficult during budget time to secure additional resources. Political leaders are much more willing to get along with the police when their constituents have a positive image of the department. One way of enhancing the public image of the police department is to ensure that it is representative of the public it serves. When historically under-represented groups see "one of their own" in a police uniform it instills confidence in their police department. Conversely, when historically under-represented groups cannot point to a person like them who has found success in a policing career then the department may be considered little more than an "army of occupation."

Finding Diversity in Your Own Backyard

Diversity is not a commodity that can be bought and sold. It is a paradigm. Although it may satisfy a pressing need, merely hiring individuals from various racial or ethnic groups does not achieve true diversity. As previously mentioned, just because a person is a racial minority does not mean that they will be an advocate for individuals or groups like themselves. In fact, it is quite unlikely that a newly hired individual will have the reputation or skill to advocate effectively for individuals who share his perspective within the department's decision-making process.

True diversity is a contract of sorts between a department and the public it serves. Departments who truly embrace diversity have enough confidence in themselves to allow and seriously consider multiple, even conflicting, perspectives when making important decisions. Diversity starts when decision makers are both aware of and actively seek a diversity of perspectives throughout the community.

Appoint an Ad Hoc Committee

One of the advantages of the racial profiling controversy is that it has encouraged police departments to form citizens' committees. Mostly, these committees are charged with designing a stop data collection project, supervising the data analysis or with writing a racial profiling policy. A few of these committees have been given the authority to evaluate racial profiling complaints and disciplinary decisions. What this has done has allowed historically under represented individuals and groups access to the police decision-making process. Often in doing so chronic critics of the police learn the complexity of the policing function and eventually become advocates for the police department. Recognizing the value of this diversity, many police departments have formalized these committees and included them in routine operational decision making.

Invest in Promising Talent

Just a few years ago nearly every police department in America sponsored a Law Enforcement Explorer Post, many still do. These programs, co-sponsored by the Boy Scouts of America, are fruitful recruiting tools. These and similar youth programs can also be used to cultivate diversity. By reaching out to and even targeting youth from historically under-represented groups the department reaps two benefits – one immediate and the other long term. The immediate benefit is that parents tend to support their children's activities as well as develop a favorable impression of the sponsoring organization. In the long term these organizations provide a department with access to future talent. Police departments often report difficulty with hiring a diverse workforce because of pay, benefits, working conditions, public image and other issues. Providing youth program participants with real opportunities to "grow into the career" will attract applicants who might otherwise not be successful in the traditional hiring process. Such programs might even include scholarships and salaried pre-service training.

Train Diversity

American policing has consistently relied on training to overcome its challenges. In most states pre-service training requirements represent hundreds of hours. Annual training requirements are common. Nearly every force strategy (firearms, batons, TASERs, etc.) requires regular proficiency training to maintain appropriate certifications and reduce liability. Some training subjects are even required by statute. Some states require annual cultural diversity training. The police rely on training and for good reason. It works. There is considerable documentation supporting the notion that officers actually use their training, especially during stressful situations. The obvious conclusion is that organizational change can be achieved through appropriate training.

But what kind of training is effective for reducing potential problems related to racial profiling? Here are a few suggestions.

–The training program should encourage officers to understand how their behavior (including their choice of words) is perceived by others. Some gestures and words are considered threatening and even offensive to some people. When officers are aware of this then they at least have the opportunity to develop alternative interpersonal communications strategies. Often the mere realization that not all people are raised with the same values or share the same life experiences, is enough to enable officers to understand that their behavior is interpreted differently by others.

–Any training program should be tailored to the specific needs of the department. If the bulk of racial profiling allegations arise from routine traffic stops then the training should focus within that context.

–The training program should transcend all aspects of the curriculum. If the objective of an annual training program is to improve the officers' cultural awareness then this teaching element should be present, to the extent it is relevant, throughout the curriculum.

–The training should involve more than sensitivity or "feel good" topics. It is simply not enough to inform officers that "people are different." They likely already know that. The reason we cannot "all just get along" is that we really don't know what 'getting along' looks like. Instead the training should demonstrate how cultural differences manifest themselves in specific behaviors and conflicts.

–The training should have a broad intellectual or theoretical basis. Any program that merely intends to teach officers how to get along with a particular type of person (i.e., racial or ethnic group) is of limited value. The objective is to teach officers how to recognize cultural differences and to respond to them appropriately, regardless of what culture is involved.

–The program's claims of effectiveness should be substantiated by objective research. Such research must have been conducted (and funded) independent from the training provider.

–The training program should teach officers how to recognize specific racial profiling behaviors within their own work. For many years police trainers have relied upon situational training. Adult learning is more effective when placed within a realistic professional context.

–The training program should provide officers with specific steps for improving their cultural awareness and conflict resolution skills. Police officers are accustomed to using guidelines and lists. For example, the *Miranda* warnings and the seven step violator contact are both effective and pervasive because they are easy to implement.

10

Respond Proactively to Allegations of Racial Profiling

S everal years ago I was asked to make a presentation before a group of police chiefs interested in implementing various problem-oriented policing strategies in their departments. At the end of the presentation one of the chiefs asked me how to encourage police officers to "get out of the car and engage in proactive problem solving with citizens." Before I could muster a response, a police chief from the back row offered the following advice. "Put a blank for them to report it when they do it on their weekly report and count them the same as, or maybe even more, than a traffic stop or an arrest. Believe me if you let it be known that you are counting it, paying attention to it, and maybe even admonishing them for not doing it then they will do it." Good advice. The research consistently indicates that most employees will at least attempt to perform in ways that are consistent with the leader's desires.

If it is possible to encourage behavior by paying attention to it then the opposite is likely true. When leaders focus attention on less than desirable behaviors and respond aggressively then employees tend to avoid such behaviors. Sometimes even the suggestion that the leader is monitoring certain behaviors can result in substantial reductions of such behaviors. One way of reducing racial profiling behaviors, or at the very least communicating the leader's concern for such behaviors, is to implement a proactive response procedure.

Citizen Complaints – The Traditional (Reactive) Response

In most departments the traditional disciplinary process begins with a citizen's formal complaint. Citizens with a complaint are required to complete a formal statement in the form of a sworn affidavit. Then, and only then, is an internal investigation initiated. If the complaint is non-criminal in nature then the entire process begins and ends within the police department. If the potential for criminal sanctions exists then most departments will bifurcate the process and conduct two separate inquiries – one for internal consumption and the other as a criminal investigation potentially involving a prosecutor. In most situations the department will inform the complainant of the results of the investigation and provide a brief description of the department's disciplinary decision, if any. This process has worked well for decades.

Despite consistent calls for more citizen oversight, the police, like many other professionals, are generally quite capable of policing themselves. Regrettably, however, this process includes some important barriers.

First, from the citizen's perspective, the formal complaint process is intimidating. Usually the process begins with a written statement from the complainant in the form of a sworn affidavit. The penalty for false swearing is normally prominently displayed on the complaint form. There is a practical reason for this formality. Because of the nature of their work, police officers are more susceptible to complaints than other professionals. Sometimes, citizens lodge complaints merely to divert attention away from their own transgressions or simply because they can. Because internal affairs resources are typically limited, there is a need to maintain a gate-keeping protocol so that only legitimate complaints are investigated. Unfortunately, even well-intentioned citizens are likely deterred from complaining out of a fear that they may unintentionally misrepresent or simply forget key facts, and in doing so put themselves at risk of prosecution.

Second, from the citizen's perspective, the complaint process is onerous. In most cases, citizens are required to appear in person at the police station, swear out a complaint form, and submit to a taped interview with an investigator before a complaint will be investigated. In addition, during this initial meeting many complainants are told that an investigator will meet with them in the future and that they may have to testify in court or at a hearing. The process is often time-consuming and burdensome to the point that some citizens, even those with legitimate concerns, will likely choose not to bother.

In contrast to how complaints are received and investigated in other professions, the citizen's complaint process in many police departments seems rather bureaucratic. For example, a few years ago my daughter came home from school rather upset that a teacher had accused her of plagiarism. The next day I telephoned the principal and asked him to look into it. He agreed and after a couple of hours he telephoned and informed me that the matter had been resolved as a simple misunderstanding. No affidavit was filed, no formal investigation was conducted and the entire process only cost me a few moments on the telephone.

Third, not all citizens have equal confidence that the police will take their complaint seriously. The vast majority of citizens' complaints are investigated thoroughly and fairly. Again, the police do a very good job of policing their own. But not everyone shares this opinion. While the research consistently indicates that the majority of all citizens regardless of their race or ethnicity tend to support the police, the level of confidence in the police department is measurably lower within the minority community. This lower level of confidence presents a special problem to the racial profiling controversy. If the department is serious about responding to racial profiling and/or the perception of racial profiling then input from the minority community is essential.

Fourth, some citizens may fear retaliation. Some citizens may question the validity of the notion that the police are capable of disciplining one of their own without reprisal in the form of increased police surveillance of their behavior or future intimidation. Incidents of police officers retaliating against complainants are exceedingly rare; however, only one is enough to create apprehension. Objective reality is not nearly as pervasive as subjective perception.

Racial Profiling Complaints – A Proactive Response

One way of responding to a controversy that threatens to adversely affect an organization is to increase administrative attention on it. American policing has a long history of success in this regard. When a police officer uses force or initiates a vehicular chase he is required to inform his supervisors rather quickly, sometimes even while the event is happening. In doing so, the officer provides the department's administration with an opportunity to intervene very quickly and make corrections if necessary. These additional and enhanced reporting requirements are specifically designed to control those behaviors that expose the department to public ridicule and even litigation.

Similar policies and procedures can be effectively used in response to allegations of racial profiling. The overall objective should be to accelerate, but not circumvent, the department's existing citizen's complaint policies and procedures. In no case should an officer's procedural rights be violated. Furthermore, the nature of an allegation should not lower the level of proof necessary to sustain a complaint.

The features of a proactive response policy when dealing with a racial profiling allegation are as follows:

– *Citizen complaints alleging racial bias or profiling may be accepted and acted upon regardless of the manner in which they are received.* This means an investigation can be initiated without requiring a complainant to appear in person, produce a sworn affidavit or submit to a taped interview.

– *Allegations of racial bias, profiling or discrimination may be accepted anonymously and acted upon.*

– *Citizen complainants should be informed of the difficulties associated with sustaining allegations of racial bias, profiling or discrimination.* Furthermore, a citizen should be encouraged to produce evidence of *racial animus* (intentional discrimination) in the form of statements, comments or other behaviors.

– *As a general rule, the department should respond to each citizen alleging racial profiling, bias or discrimination within 24 hours even at the expense of delaying work on other cases.*

– *Police officers should be required to proactively inform their supervisors when a citizen alleges racial profiling, bias or discrimination during a police/citizen encounter.* Supervisors should in turn respond promptly to the citizen to seek additional information and offer the opportunity to file a formal complaint.

– *Internal information systems (e.g., stop data describing the details of stops and the individuals stopped by that officer, videotape record systems, etc.) should be available to enable investigators to evaluate an individual officer's enforcement behaviors.*

– *Regular (at least annually) summary reports should be published describing the department's performance while investigating these reports.*

Ultimately, the features of a proactive policy will be governed by state statutes and existing labor agreements. While such a policy may be quite controversial, the need for a proactive response is well established. The racial profiling controversy is a substantial threat to the effectiveness of American policing and the entire criminal justice system. It cannot be ignored. Racial profiling, real or imagined, is as threatening to a police department as unchecked high speed chases and uncontrolled incidents of deadly force.

Final Thoughts

R eal or imagined, racial profiling is a threat to the effectiveness of American policing and likely the entire criminal justice system. Few reasonable police administrators would discount the importance of community involvement in the criminal justice process. We rely on the public to call us when crime occurs, to step up and offer witness statements, to serve on juries and to take an active part in their own public safety. Likewise, one would think it reasonable that the public would welcome police officers and recognize the inherent value of the policing function. The fact is, however, some people don't like the police. While their dislike may very well be based on subjective or even false perceptions, when an organization is perceived to be a threat it is reasonable for people to view it unfavorably. Such perceptions are likely partially responsible for the Stop Snitching Campaign in many urban communities. This grassroots effort, complete with merchandise, is designed to discourage inner city youth from reporting crime or otherwise participating in public safety. It would be unfair to blame the racial profiling controversy alone for this social malady. There is no shortage of other events that drive a wedge between the police department and certain segments of our society. It is a safe bet, however, that to the extent American policing fails to address the racial profiling controversy in a proactive and ethical way it risks losing access to a growing proportion of the American public that in many ways could benefit from positive police intervention.

Few controversies in American policing have the endurance of racial profiling. The lack of *actual proof* that large numbers of police officers are intentionally and routinely targeting racial and ethnic minorities does not seem to deter critics of the police like the ACLU's Chandra Bhatnagar from making definitive statements like "Racial profiling remains a widespread and pervasive problem throughout the U.S., impacting the lives of millions of people in the African American, Asian, Latino, South Asian, Arab and Muslim communities ..."

The racial profiling controversy began within the context of the traffic stop. When it started many police administrators merely shrugged it off as a momentary distraction. Since then, allegations of racial profiling have occurred in other contexts. Driving while Black evolved into Flying while Arab after the 9/11 tragedy. Racial and ethnic minorities have accused inattentive department store clerks as well as attentive department store security officers of profiling. Physicians have been accused of profiling while making diagnoses despite the fact that some diseases are more or less common within certain racial and ethnic groups. Racial profiling allegations have surfaced in public housing, criminal sentencing, mortgage lending practices, and many other contexts. Even a police dog has been accused of racial profiling. And at least one social commentator has opined that Tareq and Michaele Salahi would not have been able to crash a White House state dinner had they not been white.

The American humorist Mark Twain is credited with saying, "History doesn't repeat itself – at best it sometimes rhymes." Longevity in a profession sometimes affords one an ability to recognize the beginnings of a perilous path. Here is an example.

The U.S. Immigration and Customs Enforcement (ICE) agency is taking advantage of a 14-year-old law, commonly called the 287(g) program, allowing it to "deputize" state and local police officers. Upon completion of a four-week training program, a local officer would be authorized to conduct federal immigration investigations.

Touted as a supplemental enforcement tool, the program would allow local police officers ostensibly to go about their regular duties until they happen to encounter a suspected immigration violator. They then would conduct a cursory investigation possibly leading to a federal deportation proceeding.

State and local police officers have always had the authority to hold suspected immigration violators. Few departments encourage immigration holds, however, because they consume substantial resources and seldom result in deportation.

Under this program, while a local officer is conducting an immigration investigation, he would not be out on the street and responding to calls for service from local taxpayers. Of course, it is a good deal for ICE. Marcy Forman, the director of ICE's Office of Investigations, says that the program expands enforcement of federal immigration laws beyond the 5,600 ICE special agents. For local taxpayers, however, this program is little more than an abdication of federal responsibility.

While the program is intended to be supplemental, it likely will become a primary enforcement focus. A local officer with federal jurisdiction will have the legal authority to stop drivers who appear to be immigration violators. How would an officer do that without illegally considering an individual's ethnicity prior to a traffic stop?

Given the recent hysteria over "sanctuary cities," how long will it be before local agencies set up special immigration task forces? We are already there. In April 2008 the Maricopa County (Ariz.) Sheriff's Office was given local taxpayer dollars to hire 15 new deputies whose primary job is to arrest undocumented residents. Maricopa Sheriff Joe Arpaio, America's Toughest Sheriff, is now embroiled in a rather nasty lawsuit, including a U.S. Department of Justice inquiry, over the implementation of this program in his jurisdiction.

Here is the rhyming part. About 20 years ago, the U.S. Drug Enforcement Administration trained state and local officers how to use their drug courier profile to increase seizures of illegal drugs. As in the ICE 287(g) program, local officers were encouraged to use drug interdiction as a supplemental enforcement strategy.

Unfortunately, this was quickly ignored. Some officers truncated the profile and used it proactively to identify prospective drug couriers. Then, after observing a prospective drug courier commit a minor traffic violation, they initiated a traffic stop, followed closely by a search of the car. In some jurisdictions this resulted in unprecedented increases in stops involving racial and ethnic minorities and contributed substantially to the current racial profiling controversy. Maybe the Spanish writer George Santayana was right: "Those who cannot remember the past are condemned to repeat it."

Racial profiling litigation is likely to increase within the next few years. While a member of the Illinois State Legislature, Barack Obama was a strong proponent of racial profiling legislation. During his campaign for the presidency Mr. Obama expressed his intention to do the same if elected President. U.S. Attorney General Eric Holder has already increased resources in the Department of Justice Civil Rights Division specifically to investigate allegations of racial profiling. Shortly after 2008 General Election, the Obama

Administration initiated a federal inquiry into the immigration enforcement controversy involving Sheriff Joe Arpaio in Maricopa County, Arizona, something the Bush Administration largely ignored. In short, after eight years of dormancy at the federal level, there is compelling evidence suggesting a renewed interest in racial profiling litigation.

On July 28, 2010, as this book was about to go to print, Arizona Federal District Court Judge Susan Bolton issued a temporary restraining order against the State of Arizona. This order essentially prohibits the State from implementing key portions of their new anti-illegal immigration law, Senate Bill 1070. Arizona, like the three other Border States in the Southwest along with several other states throughout the nation, appears to be frustrated with the federal government's lackluster performance at deterring illegal immigration. While the U.S. Department of Justice' argument was based on the Supremacy Clause of the United States Constitution, much of the rhetoric on Arizona's Senate Bill 1070 was about racial profiling. For their part, Arizona did amend key portions of Senate Bill 1070 to reduce the potential for racial profiling.

The controversy in Arizona is instructive for those of us interested in the racial profiling controversy. First, Arizona's, as well as other state and local government, attempts to reduce the impact of illegal immigration create yet another venue for the racial profiling controversy. To be sure, illegal immigration is a serious problem with national security, economic, civil liberty and other important implications. Given the current political climate, a solution is not likely in the near future. It is clear, however, that attempts to change and/or enforce immigration law will be met with allegations, or at the very least predictions, of racial profiling. Second, the response to Arizona's anti-illegal immigration law further demonstrates a renewed interest in racial profiling litigation. In addition to the U.S. Department of Justice' lawsuit, no fewer than five advocacy groups have filed lawsuits seeking court orders to prohibit implementation of Arizona's Senate Bill 1070. Most of these lawsuits are based on predictions that local enforcement of illegal immigration will lead to racial profiling. Many of these advocacy groups are actively seeking plaintiffs who have been stopped by police officers. This means local police agencies are likely to suffer the costs associated with these lawsuits.

The primary purpose of this book is to inform. Throughout this text I have been very careful to neither accuse nor defend any person or group who is legitimately engaged in the racial profiling controversy. There is no agenda, political correctness or social commentary. The recommendations I make are based on more than sixteen years of active research, agency consultation and litigation assistance. This text is designed to provide policing leaders with an efficient way to access objective information about the racial profiling controversy. Even so, it is entirely possible that something in this text may be considered controversial. So be it. After all, a little controversy is a good thing.

References

Alpert, G.P., Smith, M.R. and Dunham, R.G. 2003 (March). Toward a Better Benchmark: Assessing the Utility of Not-at-Fault Traffic Crash Data in Racial Profiling Research. Paper presented at Confronting Racial Profiling in the 21st Century: Implications for Racial Justice. Boston, MA: Northeastern University.

American Civil Liberties Union (June, 2009). New Report from ACLU and RWG Finds Racial Profiling Still Pervasive. Retrieved from the World Wide Web (www.aclu.org) on December 3, 2009.

Barlow, D.E. and Barlow, M.H. (2002). Racial profiling: A survey of African American police officers. *Police Quarterly* 5(3): 334-58.

Bittner, E. 1970. *The Functions of the Police in Modern Society.* Washington, DC: U.S. Government Printing Office.

Black, D. J. 1971. The social organization of arrest. Stanford Law Review 23:1050-111.

Black, D. 1976. *The Behavior of Law.* New York: Academic Press.

Black, D. 1980. *The Manner and Customs of the Police.* New York: Academic Press.

Black, D.J. & Reiss, A.J., Jr. 1970. Police control of juveniles. *American Sociological Review* 35(1): 63-77.

Carter, D.L. & Katz-Bannister, A.J. 2004. *Racial profiling: Issues and implications for police policy.* In Contemporary Policing: Controversies, challenges and Solutions, Ed. Q.C. Thurman and J. Zhao, 235-47. Los Angeles: Roxbury.

Cole, D. 1999. *No Equal Justice.* New York: New Press.

Covington, J. 2001. Round up the usual suspects: Racial profiling and the War on Drugs. In *Petit Apartheid in the United States Criminal Justice System; The Dark Figure of Racism,* ed. D. Milovanivic and K.K. Russell, 27-42. Durham, NC: Carolina Academic Press.

Donzinger, S.R. 1996. *The Real War on Crime.* New York: HarperCollins.

Engel, R.S., Calnon, J.M. & Bernard, T.J. 2002. Theory and racial profiling: Shortcomings and future directions in research. Justice Quarterly 19(2): 249-273.

Fridell, L., Lunney, R., Diamond, D., Kubu, B., Scott, M., and Laing, C. (2001). *Racially biased policing: A principled response.* Washington, DC: Police Executive Research Foundation.

Harris, D.A. (1997). Driving while Black and other traffic offenses: The supreme court and pretextual traffic stops. *Journal of Criminal Law and Criminology* 87:544-82.

Harris, D.A. 2002. *Profiles in Injustice: Why Racial Profiling Cannot Work.* New York: New Press.

Heumann, M. & Cassak, L. 2003. *Good Cop, Bad Cop: Racial Profiling and Competing Views of Justice.* New York: Peter Lang.

Jernigan, A.S. (2000). Driving while Black: Profiling in America. *Law & Psychology Review* 24:127-38.

Knowles, J., Persico, N., and Todd, P. 1999. Racial Bias in Motor Vehicle Searches: Theory and Evidence. Cambridge, MA: Working Paper Series #7449, National Bureau of Economic Research.

Lamberth, J. 1994. Revised Statistical Analysis of the Incidence of Police Stops and Arrests of Black Drivers/ Travelers on the New Jersey Turnpike Between Exits or Interchanges 1 and 3 from years 1988 through 1999. West Chester, PA: Author. Retrieved July 7, 1999, from www.lamberthconsulting.com/research_articles/asp

Lange, J.E., Blackman, K.O., and Johnson, M.B. 2001. *Speed Violation Survey of the New Jersey Turnpike.* Final Report. Calverton, MD: Public Services Research Institute.

Leitzel, J. 2001. Race and policing. *Society* 38(3): 38-42.

Lundman, R.J. & Kaufman, R.L. 2003. Driving while Black: Effects of race, ethnicity, and gender on citizen self-reports on traffic stops and police actions. *Criminology* 41(1): 195-220.

MacDonald, H. 2003. *Are Cops Racists?* Chicago; Ivan R. Doe.

Novak, K.J. 2004. Disparity and racial profiling in traffic enforcement. *Police Quarterly* 7(1): 65-96.

Pallone, N.J. and Hennessy, J.J. 1999. Blacks and whites as victims and offenders in aggressive crime in the U.S.: Myths and realities. *Journal of Offender Rehabilitation* 31(1/2):1-33.

Police Foundation 2003. *A Multi-Jurisdictional Assessment of Traffic Enforcement and Data Collection in Kansas.* Washington, DC: Author.

Quinney, R. 1980. *Class, State and Crime.* New York: Longman.

Quinton, P., Bland, N., and Miller, J. (2000) Police Stops, Decision Making and Practice. London: The Policing and Reducing Crime Unite, Research, Development and Statistics Directorate, Home Office.

Ramirez, D., McDevitt, J. and Farrell, A. 2000. *A Resource Guide on Racial Profiling Data Collection Systems: Promising Practices and Lessons Learned.* Washington, DC: United States Department of Justice, Bureau of Justice Assistance.

Rojek, J., Rosenfeld, R. and Decker, S. 2004. the influence of drivers' race on traffic stops in Missouri. *Police Quarterly* 7(1): 126-47.

Rubinstein, J. 1973. *City Police.* New York: Random House.

Schultz, M. and Withrow, B.L. (2004). Racial profiling and organizational change. *Criminal Justice Policy Review,* 15 (4), 462-485.

Smith, D.A. & Visher, C.A. 1981. Street-level justice: Situational determinants of police arrest decisions. *29 Social Problems* (2): 167-77.

Smith, M.R. and Petrocelli, M. 2001. Racial profiling? A multivariate analysis of police traffic stop data. *Police Quarterly* 4: 4-27.

Statistical Assessment Service (STATS). 1999. Race and Crime: Is "Profiling" Reasonable? Retrieved September 24, 2001, from http://www.stats.ort/newsletters/9904/profile.htm

"The Man Who Shot Liberty Valance," John Ford, Director, 1962.

Tomadkovic-Devey, D. Mason, M., & Zingraff, M. 2004. Looking for the driving while black phenomena: Conceptualizing racial bias processes and their associated distributions. *Police Quarterly* 7(1): 3-29.

Tonry, M. 1995. *Malign Neglect: Race, Crime, and Punishment in America.* New York: Oxford University Press.

United States General Accounting Office. 2000. (March). *Racial Profiling: Limited Data Available on Motorist Stops.* Washington, DC: United States General Accounting Office.

Van Maanen, J. 1974. Working the street: A developmental view of police behavior. In *The Potential for Reform of Criminal Justice,* ed. H. Jacob, 830130. Beverly Hills, CA: Sage.

Walker, S. 2003. *Internal benchmarking for traffic stop data: An early intervention system approach.* Omaha: Police Professionalism Initiative, University of Nebraska at Omaha.

Walker, S., Spohn, C., & DeLone, M. 2000. *The Color of Justice: Race, Ethnicity, and Crime in America.* Belmont, CA: Wadsworth.

Washington State Patrol. 2001. *Report to the Legislature on Routine Traffic Stop Data.* Olympia: Washington State Patrol.

Weitzer, R. & Tuck, S.A. 2002. Perceptions of racial profiling: Race, class, and personal experience. Criminology 40(2): 435-56.

Wilson, J.Q. and Kelling, G. 1982. Broken windows: The police and neighborhood safety. *Atlantic Monthly* 127: 29-38.

Wise, T. 2003. Racial profiling and its apologists. In *Annual Editions: Criminal Justice,* 27th ed., J.L. Victor and J. Naughton, 91-94. Guilford, CT: McGraw-Hill/Duskin.

Withrow, B.L. 2002. *The Wichita Stop Study.* Wichita, KS: Wichita State University, Midwest Criminal Justice Institute.

Withrow, B.L. 2006. Racial Profiling: From Rhetoric to Reason. Upper Saddle River, NJ: Prentice Hall.

Withrow, B.L. (2004). Driving while different: A potential theoretical explanation of race-based policing. *Criminal Justice Policy Review,* 15 (3), 344-364.

Withrow, B.L., Dailey, J.D. and Jackson, H. (2009). The utility of in internal benchmark strategy in racial profiling surveillance. *Justice Research and Policy,* 10 (2), 19-47.

Withrow, B.L. & Jackson, H. 2002. Race based policing: Alternatives for assessing the problem. In *Crime and Justice in America: Present Realities and Future Prospects,* 2nd ed., W.R. Palacios, P.F. Cromwell, R. Dunham, 183-90. Upper Saddle River, NJ: Prentice Hall.

Cases Cited

Brown v. City of Oneonta, 235 F. 3d 769 (2nd Cir. 2000).

Miranda v. Arizona, 384 U.S. 436 (1966).

Whren, et al. vs. United States, 517 U.S. 806 (1996).

United States v. Brignoni-Ponce, 422 U.S. 873, 95 S. Ct. 2574 (1975).

United States v. Jones, FED App. 232 (2nd Cir. 2001).

United States v. Martinez-Fuente, 428 U.S. 543 (1976).

United States v. Montero-Camaro, 208 F. 3rd 1122 (9th Cir. 2000).

Index